P9-CES-664

LO: UPRISING. Contains material originally published in magazine form as HALO: UPRISING #1-4 and MARVEL SPOTLIGHT: HALO. First printing 2009. ISBN# 978-0-7851-2838-0. Published by MARVEL PUBLISHING, ., a subsidiary of MARVEL ENTERTAINMENT, INC. OFFICE OF PUBLICATION: 417 5th Avenue, New York, NY 10016. $24.99 per copy ne U.S. (GST #R127032852); Canadian Agreement #40668537. **Printed in the U.S.A**. ALAN FINE, CEO Marvel Publishing Division and EVP & CMO Marvel Characters B.V.; DAN BUCKLEY, President of lishing - Print & Digital Media; JIM SOKOLOWSKI, Chief Operating Officer; DAVID GABRIEL, SVP of Publishing Sales & Circulation; DAVID BOGART, SVP of Business Affairs & Talent Management; MICHAEL PASCIULLO, Merchandising & Communications; JIM O'KEEFE, VP of Operations & Logistics; DAN CARR, Executive Director of Publishing Technology; JUSTIN F. GABRIE, Director of Publishing & Editorial Operations; SUSAN CRESPI, orial Operations Manager; ALEX MORALES, Publishing Operations Manager; STAN LEE, Chairman Emeritus. For information regarding advertising in Marvel Comics or on Marvel.com, please contact Mitch Dane, ertising Director, at mdane@marvel.com. For Marvel subscription inquiries, please call 800-217-9158.

WRITER: Brian Michael Bendis

ARTIST: Alex Maleev

COLORISTS: Matt Hollingsworth, Jose Villarrubia & June Chung

LETTERER: Chris Eliopoulos

EDITOR: Ruwan Jayatilleke

COLLECTION EDITOR: Mark D. Beazley

ASSISTANT EDITORS: Cory Levine & John Denning

EDITORIAL ASSISTANT: Alex Starbuck

EDITOR, SPECIAL PROJECTS: Jennifer Grünwald

SENIOR EDITOR, SPECIAL PROJECTS: Jeff Youngquist

SENIOR VICE PRESIDENT OF SALES: David Gabriel

PRODUCTION: Jerry Kalinowski

BOOK DESIGNER: Spring Hoteling

EDITOR IN CHIEF: Joe Quesada

PUBLISHER: Dan Buckley

Special Thanks To:

Rich Ginter, Irene Lee, James Viscardi, Alicia Hatch, Alicia Brattin, Frank O'Connor, and Kevin Grace.

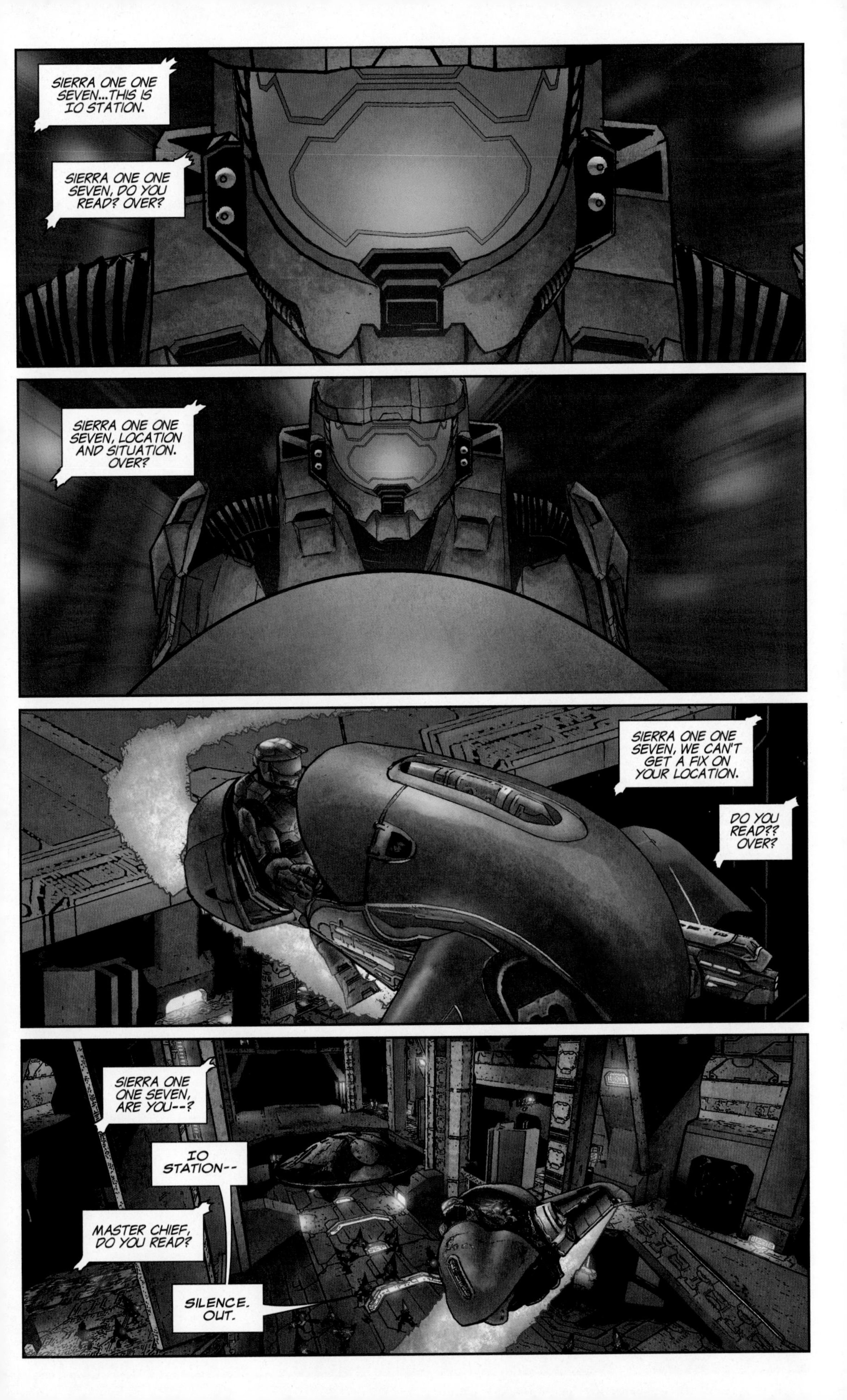
SIERRA ONE ONE SEVEN...THIS IS IO STATION.
SIERRA ONE ONE SEVEN, DO YOU READ? OVER?
SIERRA ONE ONE SEVEN, LOCATION AND SITUATION. OVER?
SIERRA ONE ONE SEVEN, WE CAN'T GET A FIX ON YOUR LOCATION.
DO YOU READ?? OVER?
SIERRA ONE ONE SEVEN, ARE YOU--?
IO STATION--
MASTER CHIEF, DO YOU READ?
SILENCE. OUT.

Aboard Forerunner Dreadnought

BRRRRRRRT
BRRRRRRRT
BRRRRRRRT
BRRRRRRRT
BRRRRRRRT

BRRRRRRRT
BRRRRRRRT
BRRRRRRRT
FABOOM

Covenant Cruiser Triumphant Declaration, Fleet of Furious Redemption
Location: Orbit of Mars
Brute Commander: Lepidus
WHO IS THIS ONE?
ACKERMON OR ACKERSON...
WHAT DIFFERENCE DOES IT MAKE? IT'S JUST ANOTHER HUMAN.
HE LED A BAND OF HUMAN TRASH AGAINST US ON THE FIELDS OF THE MARE ERYTHRAEUM.
TRUE.
THE INTERROGATION WILL CONTINUE IN THE MORN.
THE INTERROGATION IS NO LONGER NEEDED.
IT IS TO BE EXECUTED.
YOU HEAR ME, HUMAN?? YOU'RE GOING TO DIE FOR YOUR SINS.
WE'RE TAKING YOU BACK TO EARTH.
GOOD LUCK...YOU WON'T STAND A DAMN CHANCE.
WE'RE ALREADY HAVING OUR WAY WITH IT.
RIGHT NOW.
AND YOU WILL BE EXECUTED AS PART OF THE VICTORY CEREMONY.
IF YOU IDIOTS...RRR...
ATTACK EARTH...
YOU'LL NEVER FIND THE KEY.
WHAT KEY?

OPEN THE CELL.
AAAGGHH!!
WHAT KEY?
WHAT KEY?!!
AAAGGHH!!
WHAT KEY?

THE KEY--
THE ONE--
ARGH!! FROM THE--PLEASE...
I DON'T--
ALL I KNOW IS...IT'S CALLED THE KEY OF... O-OSANALAN.
I DUNNO WHAT YOU CALL IT.
AND I'M TELLING YOU--IF YOU DESTROY THE CITIES YOU'LL NEVER FIND IT.
AND IF YOU DON'T FIND IT--AGH!
ARGH!!
IF WE DON'T FIND IT WHAT?!!
I--I JUST KNOW THAT WITHOUT IT-- THE HALO WILL FAIL...
LIKE IT FAILED LAST TIME-- ARGH!!
WHERE IS IT?!!
I DON'T KNOW!!
AGGH!!
OKAY!! OKAY!!!
I KNOW-- I KNOW WHICH...
CLEVELAND!!
BUT I DON'T KNOW WHERE!!
I JUST KNOW IT'S...IN CLEVELAND.
I DON'T KNOW WHAT IT DOES-- ARH!!
I JUST KNOW IT'S THERE AND BEING GUARDED.
AND IT'S...
IT'S...
...
WHAT IS IT TALKING ABOUT?
I DON'T KNOW.
IT'S LYING. THEY LIE.
THAT'S WHAT THEY DO. THEY'RE ANIMALS.
WE NEED TO REPORT IT TO THE HIERARCHS.
CLEVE. LAND.
WHAT IS A CLEVE?

IN CLEVELAND OF ALL PLACES!
I'M GOING TO DIE TODAY??
WELL, THAT'S JUST GREAT!!

I'M GOING TO DIE IN THIS PLACE!??!! I HATE THIS PLACE!! I TRULY, PROFOUNDLY, CAN'T STAND THIS PLACE!! IF I KNEW I WAS GOING TO DIE TODAY I SURE AS #$%# WOULDN'T HAVE COME IN TO WORK!! HEY!! SOMEBODY HELP US!! SOMEBODY GET DOWN HERE WITH A TANK OR--OR A WAR-SHIP OR WHATEVER THE HELL YOU CALL THEM AND DO SOMETHING!! WHY IS THIS ALLOWED TO HAPPEN??

WHERE ARE ALL THE POLICE AND THE ARMY AND THE GUYS IN THE SUITS!!?? WHERE ARE YOU?? OH MY GOD, THEY DESTROYED MOMBASA!! I USED TO LIVE IN MOMBASA!! MY OLD APARTMENT--GONE. MY OLD FRIENDS!! I'D BE DEAD. DAMN DEAD! JENGI!! JENGI LIVED IN MOMBASA. I MEANT TO CALL HER. SHE'S PROBABLY DEAD. AND I'M GOING TO DIE. I SHOULD FIGHT THIS!!

I SHOULD DO SOMETHING TO HELP STOP THIS.

I'M A DAMN HOTEL CONCIERGE!! WHAT THE $%# CAN I DO?? I WASTED MY LIFE!!! AND I SHOULD HAVE MADE OUT WITH THAT GIRL THAT TIME. SHE WAS THROWING HERSELF AT ME!! WHAT WAS I THINKING?? HOLDING OUT FOR SOMEONE BETTER!!?? WHAT WAS HER NAME?? NOONI--NANA--NINDIA. NINDIA! THERE WAS NO ONE BETTER!! THERE WAS NOTHING. NOTHING BETTER CAME!!
THIS CAME!! THAT'S WHAT CAME!!! THIS IS IT? THIS?? WHY ARE THEY HERE?? LOOK AT ALL THE STUFF THEY HAVE!! WHY DO THEY NEED TO DO THIS?? BLOWING UP A FANCY HOTEL?? TAKING OVER A HOTEL?? YOU CAME HALFWAY ACROSS WHATEVER TO TAKE OVER A RESORT CITY?? I DON'T UNDERSTAND!! WE WEREN'T BOTHERING ANYBODY!!
WHAT ARE ALL YOU PEOPLE DOING?? WHERE ARE YOU RUNNING TO?? THERE'S NOWHERE TO RUN!! $%?#!! THIS IS NOT WHAT I WANTED OUT OF LIFE. I HATE HOTELS. I HATE PEOPLE THAT STAY IN HOTELS. I'M PRETTY SURE I HATE PEOPLE.
SO WHY DID I DO THIS FOR A LIVING?? UGH!! AAAGGHH!! SO, LET'S GO OVER THIS... I DIDN'T LIKE MY JOB, I HAVE NO GIRLFRIEND, I REALLY DON'T LIKE MY LIFE THAT MUCH...
SO WHY THE $%?$ DO I WANT TO--??
UM, EXCUSE ME, DO YOU HAVE A GUN I COULD BORROW?

WE NEED TO GET SOME GUNS.
ARE THERE ANY IN THE BACK?
UH...
NO.
YOU'RE A CONCIERGE!! YOU DON'T KNOW WHERE TO GET GUNS?
NO!!
IS THE SECURITY GUARD AROUND?
I DON'T KNOW.
YOU **DO** SEE WHAT'S GOING ON OUTSIDE, RIGHT?

JEEZ!!
WE'RE GOING TO DIE.
SHUT UP.
WE'RE GOING TO DIE!!
THEY'RE DESTROYING THE WORLD!!
YEAH? WELL, MY BOYFRIEND LEFT ME HERE.
WE'RE NEXT!!
HE TAKES ME ALL THE WAY HERE FROM PARIS FOR A GETAWAY AND THEN THIS HAPPENED AND HE-- HE JUST GOT IN A JEEP AND LEFT.
CAN YOU IMAGINE?
HE DOESN'T EVEN TRY TO TAKE ME WITH HIM! I'M GOING TO KILL HIM.
HE'S PROBABLY DEAD.

GO TO HELL!!
STOP!!
YOU DON'T-- ARGH!!
FSHAMM
CLUMP
WHOAH.
GUNS.
HERE!
WHAT?
NO!

YOU GOT A CAR??
UH--
A CAR!!
IN THE PARKING GAR--
LET'S GO.
HUAGH!!
OH MY GOD!!! OH MY GOD!!! OH MY GOD!!!
THIS IS AN INSANE PERSON!!

SHE DOES LOOK FAMILIAR.
DO I KNOW YOU FROM--?
WHAT IS IT?? WHAT'S HAPPENING??
WHAT'S HAPPENING?? CRACK A WINDOW!! TAKE A PEEK!!
WHICH WAY?
UH, UH...
THE DOOR. THAT DOOR.
I DO. I KNOW THIS WOMAN. DID I HELP HER WHEN SHE CHECKED IN? IS THAT IT? I'M SHAKING. I'M SHAKING SO HARD, I CAN'T--
CALM DOWN!!
GARAGE
OH MY GOD! DO YOU SEE THAT??
DO I SEE IT?
JUST--WHERE ARE WE GOING??
WHICH ONE?
THE RED ONE.
THIS IS YOUR CAR? HOW OLD ARE YOU?
OH MY GOD. OH MY GOD, OH MY GOD!! OKAY, OKAY, WE'LL DRIVE TO THE UNDERGROUND PASS, THEN WE'LL--
HOLD ON-- JUST A SECOND.
WHO ARE YOU?
I'VE--I'VE NEVER DONE ANYTHING LIKE THAT BEFORE.
I DON'T KNOW WHERE TO GO.
RUWAN!!

DORI!??!! ARE YOU--?? WHERE ARE YOU GOING??
THE ROADS ARE GONE!! THERE'S NO WAY OUT.
ARE YOU SURE?? EVEN THE UNDERGROUND PASS??
WE JUST CAME FROM THERE!!
WHERE ARE YOU GOING??
THE ROADS ARE GONE!!!
WHERE ARE YOU GOING??
I DON'T KNOW WHAT TO DO.
WHAT WAS YOUR NAME AGAIN?
WHERE ARE YOU GOING??

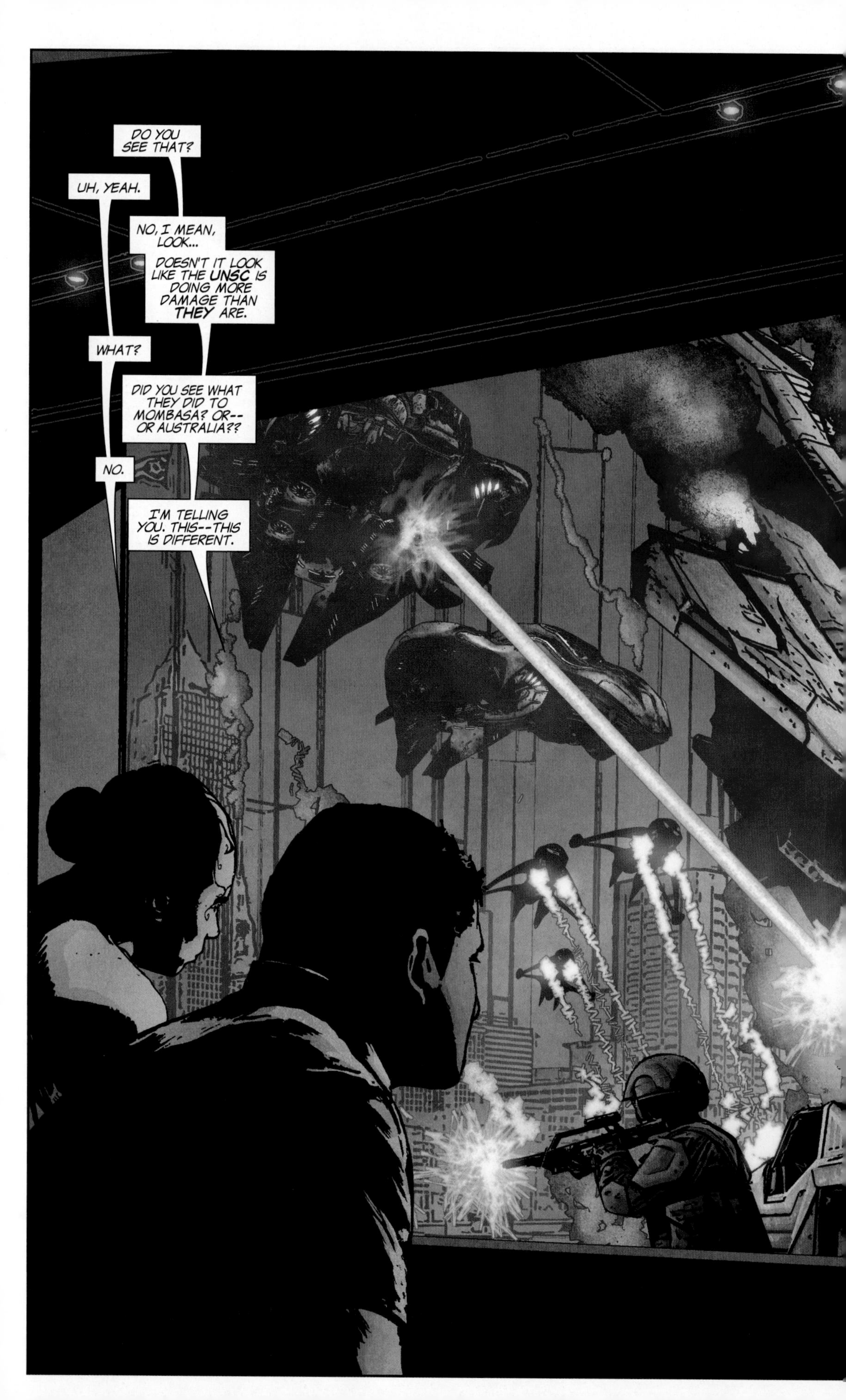
DO YOU SEE THAT?
UH, YEAH.
NO, I MEAN, LOOK...
DOESN'T IT LOOK LIKE THE **UNSC** IS DOING MORE DAMAGE THAN **THEY** ARE.
WHAT?
DID YOU SEE WHAT THEY DID TO MOMBASA? OR-- OR AUSTRALIA??
NO.
I'M TELLING YOU. THIS--THIS IS DIFFERENT.

THEY'RE NOT DESTROYING US.
WELL, IT KIND OF LOOKS LIKE THEY ARE.
LOOK!
THEY DESTROYED MOMBASA.
I THINK--IT LOOKS LIKE THEY'RE INVADING US.
THIS-- THIS MIGHT BE WORSE.
OH WELL...THAT IS AN INTERESTING THEORY...
ON THE OTHER HAND...
LOOK AT WHAT IS HAPPENING!!

WELL, UH, THANKS FOR, UM--
I GOT TO GO.
WAIT!! WHERE ARE YOU GOING?

I DON'T KNOW.
I--I DON'T EVEN KNOW WHERE I AM!!
DON'T-- DON'T LEAVE.

WHAT?
WHATEVER, BOY, WE'RE PRETTY CLOSE TO DEAD EITHER WAY!!
I ALWAYS THOUGHT IT WAS ALL PROPAGANDA.
THE WAR.
IT'S SOMETHING THEY KEEP OUT THERE TO KEEP THE MILITARY-INDUSTRIAL COMPLEX IN BUSINESS.
LOOK AT THE MONEY THEY SPEND ON ALL THIS.
I WAS AN ART MAJOR.
I DON'T KNOW WHAT THE $$#% I'M TALKING ABOUT.
WE'LL SURRENDER!!
LISTEN, EVERYONE!! WE'LL SURRENDER, THEY'LL RESPECT THAT.
WELL, WE CAN'T STAY HERE.
THERE'S GOT TO BE A WAY OUT OF THIS CITY.
WAIT!
THE BOATS.
CANADA.

OLD CLEVELAND.
I'M GOING TO PUKE UP MY OWN FEET.
WOW. WHAT IS THAT SMELL?
OLD CLEVELAND.
I THINK I MAY PUKE UP MY OWN FEET.
WHERE ARE WE GOING?
THE SEWERS.
WHERE ARE THEY?
UNDERNEATH US.
SHIT.
SSHH.

WHAT DO YOU DO?
DO?
FOR A LIVING.
OH, UH, I PLAY THE STYLLIGHT.
OH, YOU'RE MYRAS TYLA.
YEAH.
I KNEW I KNEW YOU.
YOU HELPED CHECK ME INTO THE HOTEL.
I HAVE SOME OF YOUR WORK.
WE HAVE TO GET OFF THE STREET.
ONE OF THESE FLAMING DEATH-SHIPS IS GOING TO LAND RIGHT ON OUR--

N--
DON'T!!
WE'RE--WE'RE NOT--OKAY.
JUST DON'T--

PLEASE, WE DON'T EVEN KNOW WHAT YOU WANT FROM US!!
JUST TELL US WHAT YOU WANT!!
WHAT DO YOU WANT FROM US??
SPOK
AGH!
JUST TELL US WHAT YOU WANT!!

BRRRRRRRT
BRRRRRRRT
SHAAAA
BRRRRRRRT
BRRRRRRRT
FSHAMMMM
FSHAMMMM
FSHAMMMM
FSHAMMMM

FSHAMMMM
FSHAMMMM
FSHAMMMM
FSHAMMMM
FSHAMMMM
FSHAMMMM
FSHAMMMM
TOOM
CEASE FIRE, UNGGOY!!
I SAID, CEASE FIRE!!

DEMON.
THE KEY OF OSANALAN.
YOU'RE GOING TO GIVE IT TO US.
TINK TINK
WE'LL START PULLING PARTS OFF OF YOU UNTIL YOU DO.

KACHUNK
OUT!!
OUT!!
MOVE!!!
MOVE!!
WHERE ARE YOU TAKING US?? PLEASE, JUST TELL US, WHERE YOU--??
MOVE!!!

YOU ARE NOW PRISONERS OF WAR!!
YOU ARE BEING KEPT ALIVE BY THE GENEROSITY OF THE PROPHETS!!
IF YOU WOULD LIKE TO SEE YOUR LIVES CONTINUE, YOU WILL GIVE US WHAT WE CAME HERE FOR!!

THE KEY OF OSANALAN.
YOU WILL BRING IT FORWARD, YOU WILL LEAD US TO IT.
AND YOU WILL BE ALLOWED TO LIVE.
YOU WILL BE REWARDED!!

THE WHAT? WHAT DID HE SAY?
THE KEY...OF OSANALAN.
WHAT IS THAT?
I--
I KNOW EXACTLY WHAT IT IS.

SIERRA ONE ONE SEVEN--CAN I GET A RADIO CHECK--OVER?
DEMON!!
DEMON, CAN YOU HEAR ME IN THERE??
ABOARD FORERUNNER DREADNOUGHT
DEMON!!
SIERRA ONE ONE SEVEN--SAY AGAIN--OVER.
THE KEY OF OSANALAN.
WHERE IS IT?
WHAT DOES OSANALAN MEAN???

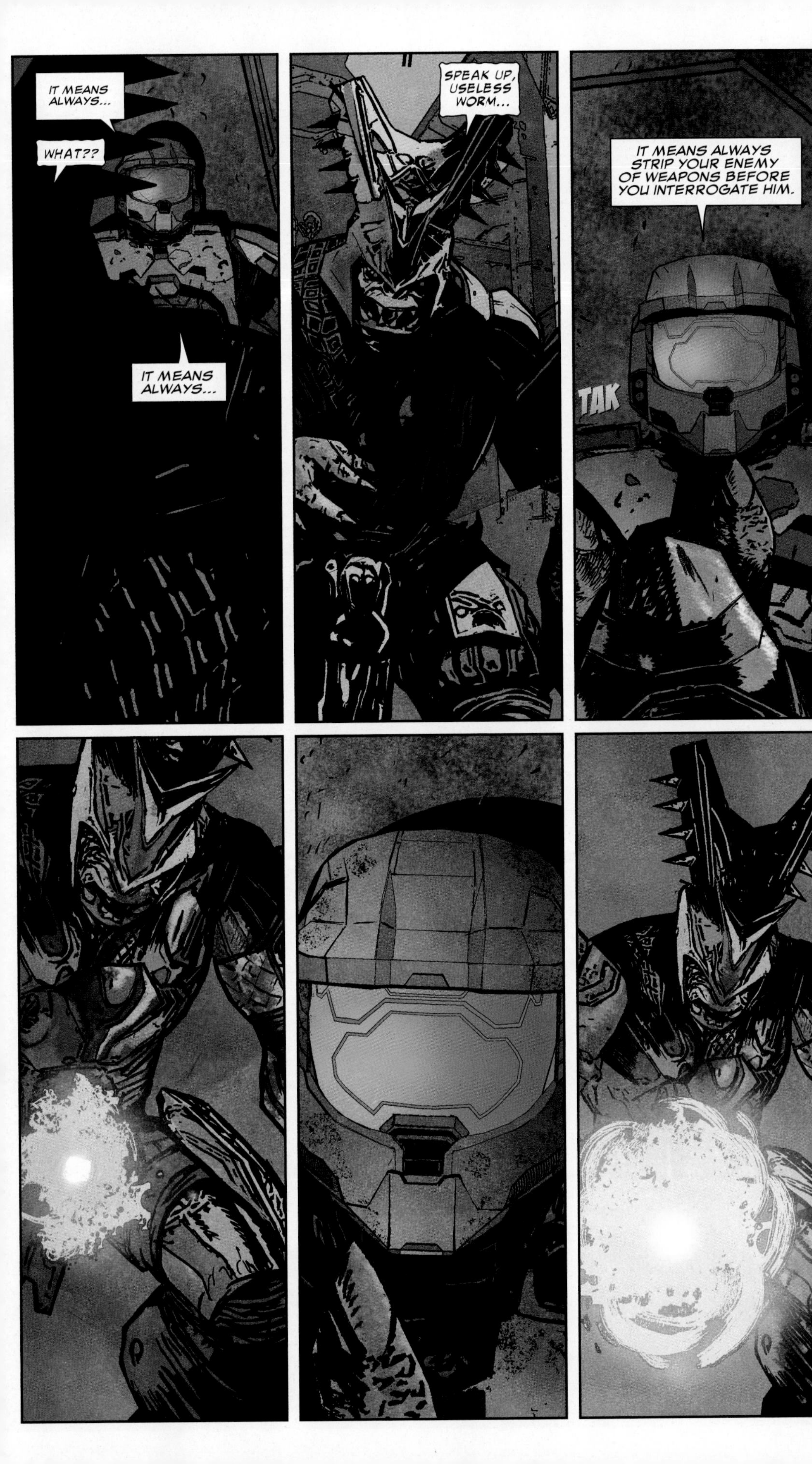
IT MEANS ALWAYS...
WHAT??
IT MEANS ALWAYS...
SPEAK UP, USELESS WORM...
IT MEANS ALWAYS STRIP YOUR ENEMY OF WEAPONS BEFORE YOU INTERROGATE HIM.
TAK

ANY SIGN OF THE WRETCHED HUMAN?
ANY SIGN OF THE DEMON??!!

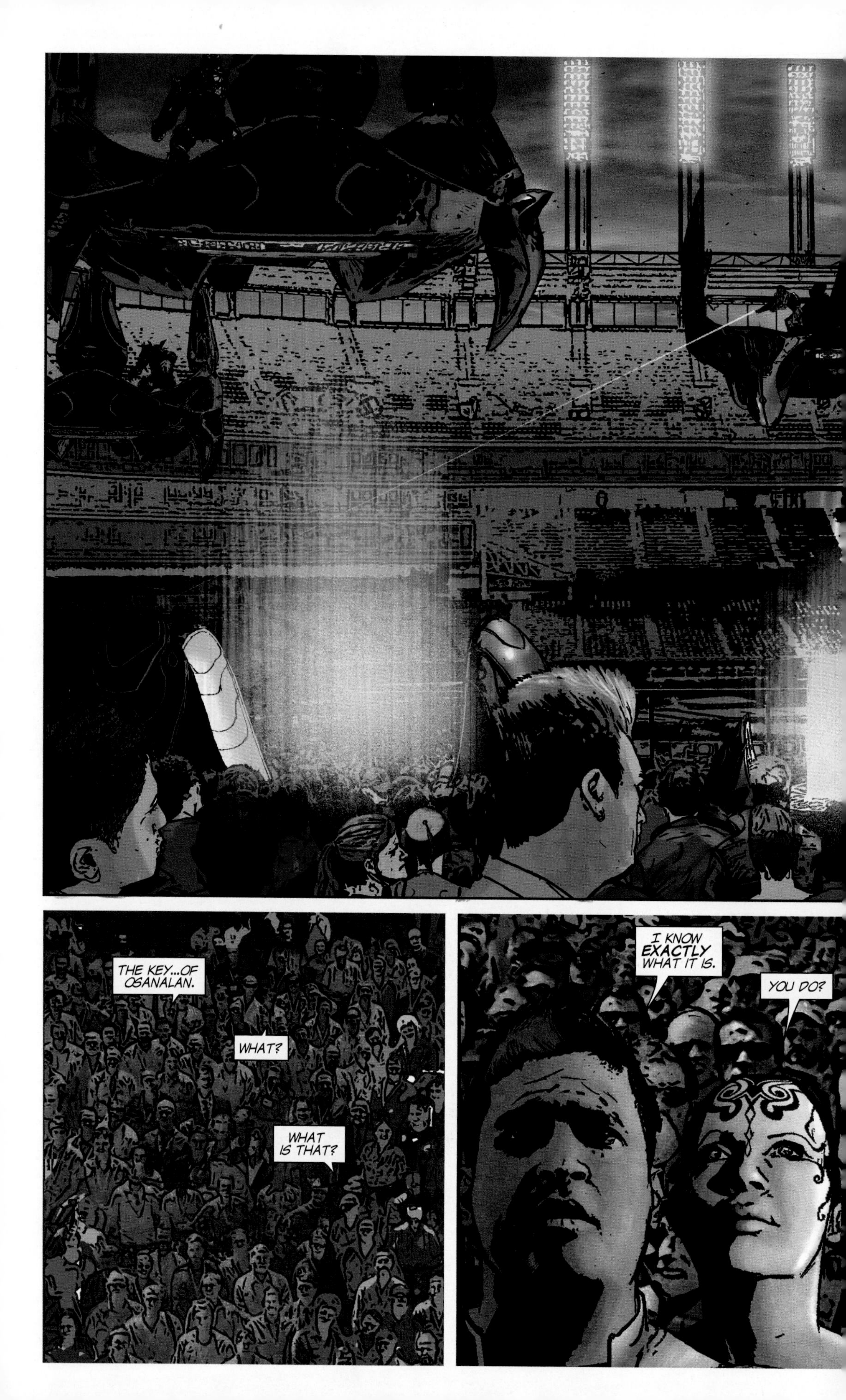
THE KEY...OF OSANALAN.
WHAT?
WHAT IS THAT?
I KNOW EXACTLY WHAT IT IS.
YOU DO?

CLEVELAND, OLD CITY
HUMANS!!
THE KEY OF OSANALAN.
BRING IT FORWARD AND YOU WILL FEEL THE GENEROSITY OF THE PROPHETS.
THE KEY OF OSANALAN. YOU WILL BRING IT FORWARD AND YOU WILL--
CHOOM!

THIS IS IT.
THIS IS REALLY IT.
YOU'RE DYING TODAY.

BUT, OKAY, IF THIS IS IT, YOU'LL BE OUT THERE.
YOUR WORK IS OUT THERE. YOU'LL BE REMEMBERED.
OH MY GOD!!
I- I-
I DON'T WANT TO DIE!! I DIDN'T DO ANYTHING, WHY IS THIS HAPPENING??

I REALLY SCREWED IT ALL UP. MY DAD WAS RIGHT. #@#$ HIM!! HE WAS RIGHT. I SHOULD HAVE WRITTEN MORE OF MY OWN MUSIC. I SHOULD HAVE WRITTEN EVERY DAY. WRITERS WRITE. WHAT THE ##$% WAS I DOING?? I WAS POSING IN HALF MY CLOTHES FOR MAGAZINES AND COVERS. I SHOULD HAVE LET MY MUSIC SPEAK FOR ITSELF INSTEAD OF SHOWING MY TITS AND ASS EVERY TIME A PHOTOGRAPHER ASKED ME TO.

I SHOULDN'T HAVE DONE THOSE KID'S SHOWS. I DIDN'T WANT KIDS LISTENING TO MY MUSIC. I DON'T WANT TO MAKE MUSIC KIDS WOULD WANT. I SOLD MYSELF LIKE A WHORE TO CHILDREN AND NOW THIS IS IT!!

THAT'S HOW I'LL BE REMEMBERED. I'LL BE DEAD AND HALF NAKED IN SOME SOLDIER'S LOCKER ON SOME SPACE STATION SOMEWHERE I'VE NEVER EVEN HEARD OF BECAUSE THE WHOLE ENTIRE EARTH WILL NO LONGER BE FOR HUMANS AND THAT ASS WON'T EVEN HAVE EVEN LISTENED TO MY MUSIC.

I NEVER FINISHED "DEAD FLOWERS." IT COULD HAVE BEEN THE ONE. IT COULD HAVE BEEN MY "JULI NIGHTS."

WHAT IF I DIDN'T HAVE ANYTHING TO SAY? WHAT IF I WAS JUST ONE OF THOSE PEOPLE? NOT EVERYONE HAS A PROFOUND VIEW OF THE WORLD AND I WAS RICH AT 17 YEARS OLD. MAYBE I JUST DIDN'T HAVE THAT THING IN MY HEART. MAYBE I WASN'T THE ARTIST I THOUGHT I WAS. MAYBE I WAS JUST TITS AND ASS.

I WANTED TO DO MORE. I WANTED TO BE IN LOVE. I WANTED SOMEONE TO JUST GET ME AND WANT THE BEST FOR ME.

PHILIP, YOU #$%#ING @##HOLE, YOU LEFT ME HERE!! WHY COULDN'T I SEE THAT YOU'D BE THE KIND OF @##HOLE WHO'D LEAVE ME!! WHY WOULD I LET YOU HAVE MY BODY IF I KNEW DEEP DOWN YOU HATED ME SO MUCH. THAT YOU CARED SO #*%@ING LITTLE.

I HOPE YOU'RE DEAD!! NO, I DON'T I DON'T HOPE YOU'RE DEAD!! I HOPE YOU'RE ALIVE!! AND I'LL TELL YOU WHY??

I HOPE YOU GOT OUT OF THIS CITY SAFELY. I DO. I HOPE YOU'RE SAFE.

AND I HOPE YOU NEVER SLEEP ANOTHER NIGHT IN YOUR LIFE BECAUSE MY FACE, THE FACE OF GUILT, THE FACE OF SHAME, THE FACE OF WHAT YOU REALLY ARE...AN @#$HOLE THAT WOULD ABANDON SOMEONE AT THE FIRST SIGN OF TROUBLE, HAUNTS YOU TILL YOU'RE A HUNDRED AND TEN #$%%ING YEARS OLD.

I'LL TELL YOU THIS, PHILIP-I'M GOING TO GET OUT OF HERE!! I'M GOING TO GET OUT OF HERE AND I'M GOING TO FIND MY DAD AND I'M GOING TO MAKE MUSIC. REAL MUSIC, MUSIC THAT HASN'T BEEN MADE BEFORE, MUSIC THAT'S FOR ME, MUSIC THAT HAS NO GENRE!! I'M GOING TO PLAY WHAT I WANT AND SING WHAT I WANT AND YOU'LL NEVER GET TO TOUCH ME AGAIN. THIS ISN'T IT, I CAN FEEL IT, I'M NOT GOING TO DIE HERE, I'M NOT. I'M GETTING OUT.

I'M GOING TO PLAY MY SONGS FOR THESE PEOPLE. THIS GUY AND ME. WE HAVE TO GET MARRIED.

WE HAVE TO! WE HAVE THE BEST MEETING STORY EVER!! MOMMY, HOW DID YOU MEET DAD?? "WELL ALIEN TERRORISTS ATTACKED MY HOTEL AND YOUR DAD AND I RAN FOR OUR LIVES AND WE-"

@#$%! WHAT'S HIS NAME AGAIN?? IT'S WITH AN R- HOW DO I ASK HIM WHAT HIS NAME IS NOW??? AFTER WHAT WE'VE BEEN THROUGH?? RUGIE. RUGGLES. RUWANS. ROWANS.

RUWAN!! HE HAD A NAME TAG, RUWAN.

I COULD MARRY HIM. HE LIKES MY MUSIC. HE DIDN'T LEAVE ME.

HE IS RIGHT HERE!!
"HERE!"
WHERE IS HERE?? WHERE AM I??
SHABOOM
FABOOM
KRABOOM
BOOM
WHERE ARE WE?
OLD TOWN.
WHERE ARE WE GOING??
FABOOM
BOOM
BOOM
COME ON!!!
SCREEEEEE
BOOM
AGH!
BOOM
FABOOM
SCREEEEEE
BOOM
BOOM
OH MY GOD!!

AGH!
HOLD ON!!
#$%!
WHERE ARE WE GOING??
I DON'T KNOW.
DO YOU KNOW HOW TO DRIVE ONE OF THESE??
OF COURSE NOT!!
SCREEEEVRROOOOOOOOMM
WHOAH!!
SORRY!!
HOW ABOUT THERE?
WHERE IS THERE?

I DON'T KNOW BUT IT'S NOT WHERE WE WERE!
AND NOT WHERE WE WERE HAS TO BE GOOD.
GUESS WE MISSED THE FIGHT HERE.
YEAH. LUCKY US.
YEAH, LUCKY'S NOT THE WORD FLOATING AROUND IN MY HEAD RIGHT NOW.
SCEE
SCEE
SCEE

SO, UH, WHAT ARE WE DOING HERE?
IT'S QUIET.
I JUST- I NEED- I NEED TO HAVE A MOMENT.
YEAH, OKAY.
WE NEED TO THINK.
OKAY.
THERE'S- THERE'S A WAY OUT OF THIS, RIGHT?
SCEE SCEE SCEE
BOOM
SCEE SCEE SCEE
WHAT ARE YOU-?
VUM-WHIRRRR

CHE-OOOOOOO
SH-WRAACK!
HEY!!
WHOAH!!
I JUST-
I JUST KILLED.
I JUST KILLED SOMETHING. IT HAS A FAMILY AND I KILLED IT.
LET'S-HEY-LET'S GET INSIDE SOMEWHERE.
LET'S JUST-LET'S GO GET A HOLD OF OURSELVES.
I KILLED IT.
IT WAS GOING TO KILL YOU.
I KILLED IT.
IT WAS GOING TO KILL YOU.
COME ON.

WHEN THIS IS OVER, I'M GOING TO GET ME ONE OF THESE.
I'M SURE THE MILITARY'LL RUN RIGHT OVER.
IS THERE A RADIO?? WE CAN CALL- CALL FOR HELP.
WELL, SOMEONE'S GOT TO BE TRYING TO HELP US.
HOW ABOUT A BUTTON- WE PUSH IT AND WE TRANSPORT OUT OF HERE.
THAT WOULD BE NICE.
THERE'S NO RADIO?
MAYBE THEY HAVE THEM ON THEIR ARMOR OR SOMETHING?
BECAUSE NOW I'M AN EXPERT IN EVERYTHING. STOP TALKING. HE'S GOING TO LEAVE YOU.
HEY...
THAT'S SOMETHING.
WE CAN CHANGE. THERE'S BANDAGES.
YEAH, I KINDA WANNA CHANGE.
AND I KINDA NEED BANDAGES.
WHAT IS THAT?
IT SAYS HEAT STICK.
HEAT STICK?
COOL.
LIKE A CAMP FIRE.
A WHAT?
AGH! DAMN!!
YEAH.
IT SAID HEAT.
GIVE ME THAT SHIRT.

LOOK AT US.
LOOK AT US.
MY NAME'S RUWAN BY THE WAY.
RUWAN.
I KNOW. WAS THERE FOOD IN THERE?
IF YOU COULD CALL IT THAT.
IT WAS GOING TO KILL YOU IF IT SAW YOU.
WHAT?
THAT THING YOU KILLED.
BUT WHY WAS IT GOING TO KILL ME?
WHY ARE THEY HERE? WHY ARE THEY TRYING TO KILL US OFF??
WE'RE AT WAR.
I'M SORRY I WAS GOING TO LEAVE YOU BEFORE.
OH, IT'S OKAY. WE DON'T EVEN KNOW EACH OTHER.
BUT I WAS LEFT HERE BY MY JERK BOYFRIEND- AND I WAS GOING TO LEAVE YOU.
I WAS GOING TO DO TO YOU WHAT-
IT'S OKAY.
I'M STILL SORRY. I'M EMBARRASSED.
YOU'RE- YOU'RE IN SHOCK OR SOMETHING. WHAT WE'VE SEEN.
ARE YOU IN SHOCK?
YES.
YOU DON'T LOOK IT.
I WANT MY LIFE BACK. I HATED IT, AND NOW I WANT IT BACK.
YEAH.

RUWAN.
YEAH?
SEE? I KNOW YOUR NAME.
AND I KNOW YOURS. I HAVE YOUR MUSIC.
DO YOU REALLY?
YOU'RE REALLY GOOD. AND I'M NOT JUST SAYING THAT.
I BOUGHT YOUR LAST ONE WITH MY OWN CREDIT. IT'S ON MY RICO.
I COULD HAVE DONE MORE.
YOU HAD A CAREER, AT LEAST. I, ME, I COULD HAVE DONE MORE.
WHAT DID YOU WANT TO DO?
I DON'T KNOW. IF I DID...
WHAT ARE YOU GOOD AT?
WELL I RECENTLY DISCOVERED I'M RATHER GOOD AT RUNNING AND SCREAMING.
BUT I HAVEN'T HAD TIME TO DEVELOP IT INTO A MONEYMAKING SKILL.
WELL, I'VE THOUGHT ABOUT IT, AND I THINK WE'RE GOING TO HAVE TO GET MARRIED.
HA.
SURE. JUST FOR THE STORY.
HOW DID YOU AND MOMMY MEET, WELL, ALIENS ATTACKED THIS HOTEL DADDY WAS WORKING AT-

THEY'RE HERE!!
SSSHH!!
SHIT!
CACHUN
CACHUN
CACHUN

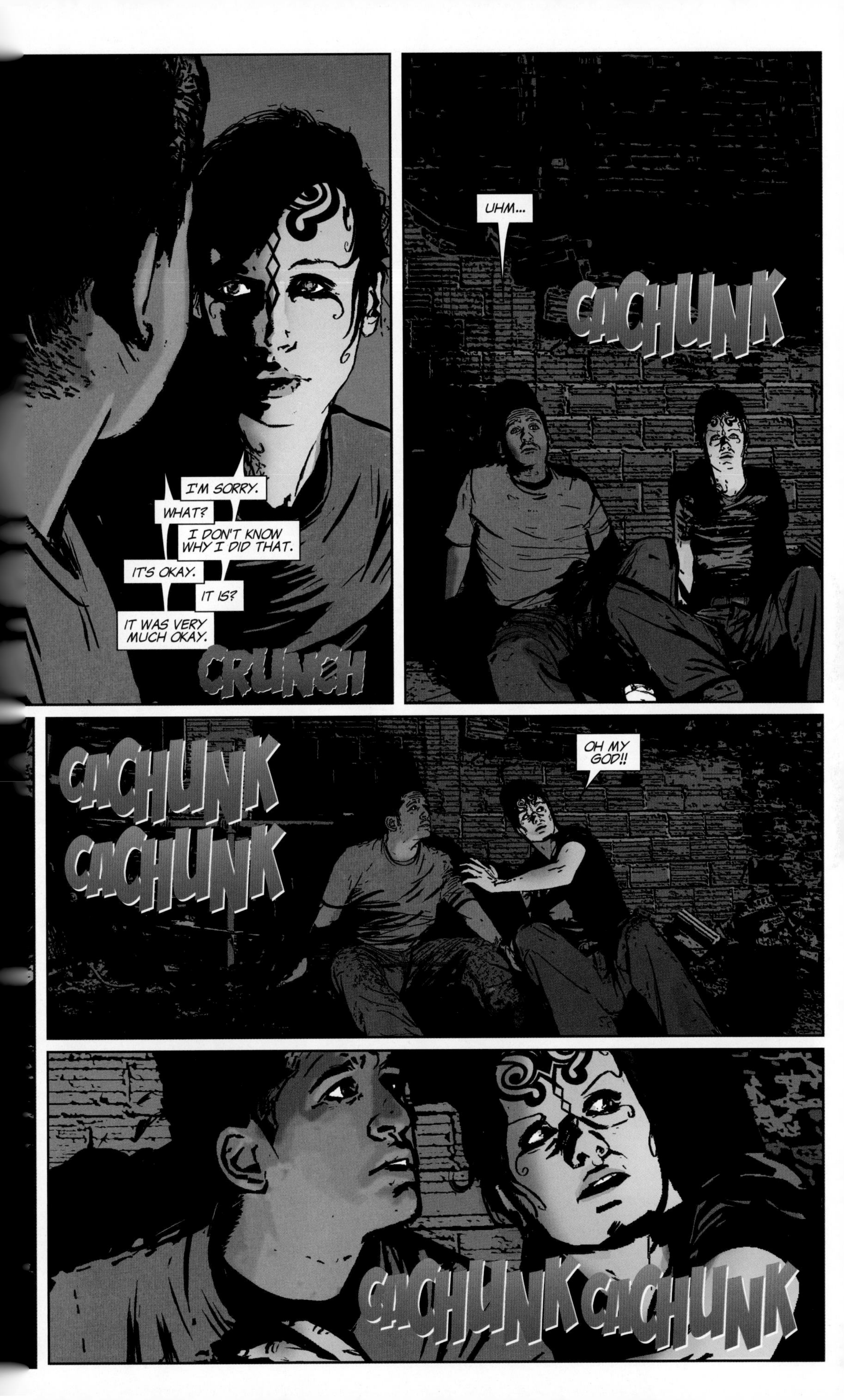
I'M SORRY.
WHAT?
I DON'T KNOW WHY I DID THAT.
IT'S OKAY.
IT IS?
IT WAS VERY MUCH OKAY.
CRUNCH
UHM...
CACHUNK
CACHUNK
CACHUNK
OH MY GOD!!
CACHUNK CACHUNK

CACHUNK
CACHUNK
CACHUNK
CACHUNK
CACHUNK
CACHUNK
CACHUNK
CACHUNK
WHAT DO THEY-

OH MY GOD!!
SSHH.
CACHUNK
CACHUNK
CACHUNK
CACHUNK
CACHUNK
CACHUNK
CACHUNK
CACHUNK
CACHUNK

GG!!
MAN!!

HEY...
WHAT DO THEY WANT???
DID YOU HEAR HIM SAY- BEFORE AT THE STADIUM- DID YOU HEAR HIM SAY THE KEY?
HE SAID THE KEY OF OSANALAN. YOU HEARD HIM, RIGHT?
YOU SAID YOU KNEW WHAT IT WAS.
I- I DO. BUT...
WHAT IS IT??
I FEEL LIKE I'M GOING INSANE...

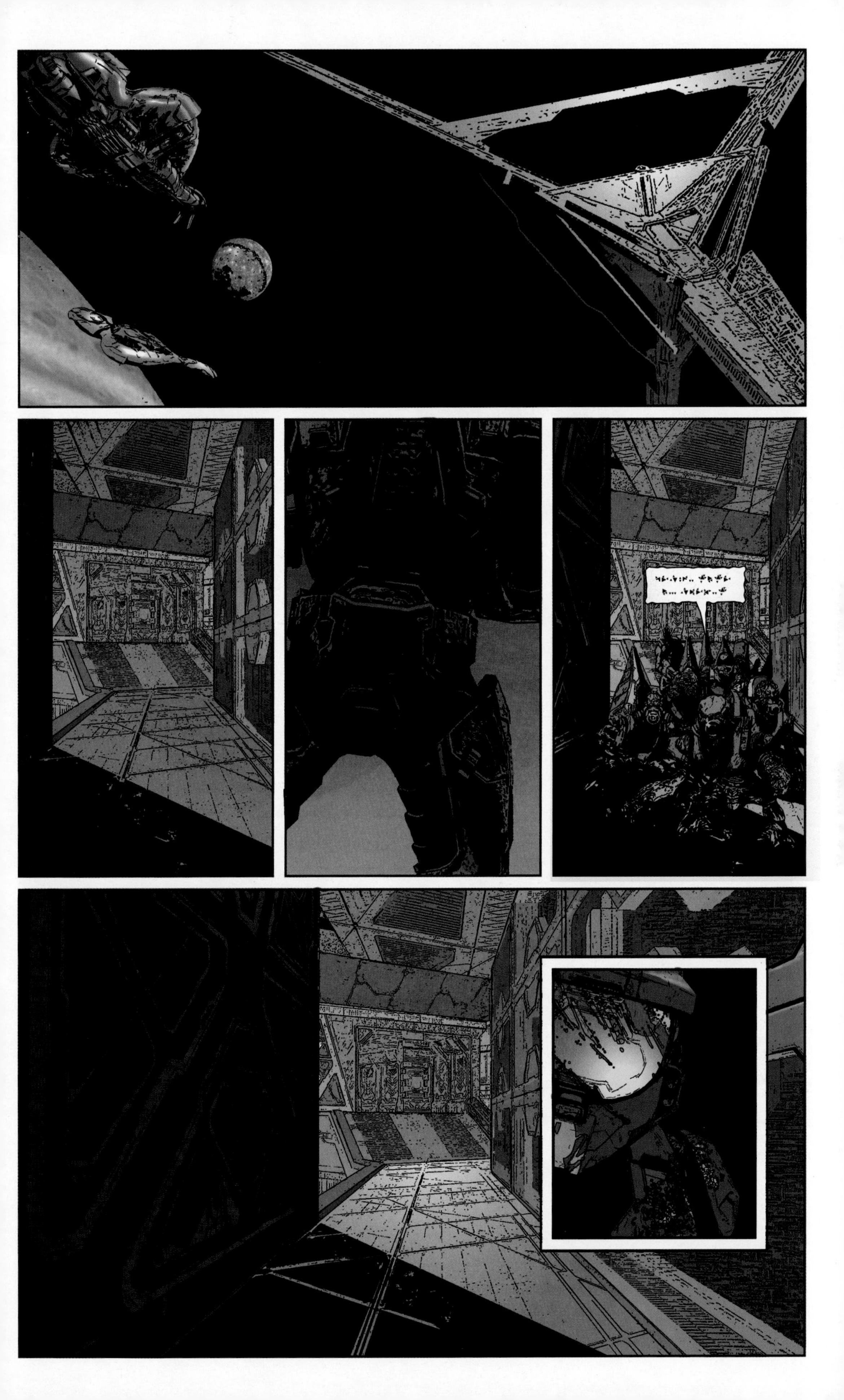

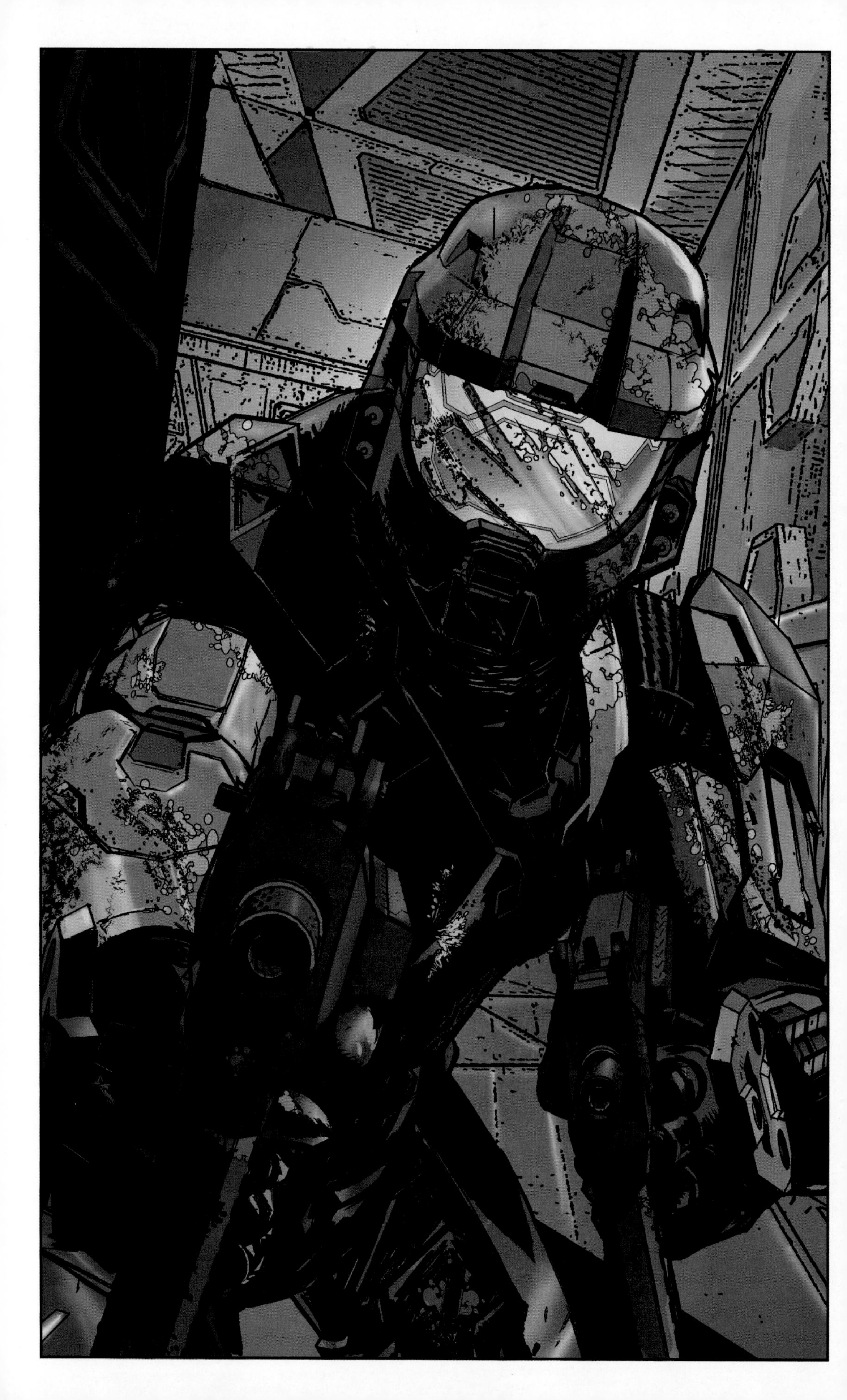

THE PROPHET OF TRUTH
AND HIS GUARDS

IO STATION-CONFIRM RECEIPT OF KEY OF OSANALAN TRANSMISSION-OVER.
CONFIRMED! KEY OF OSANALAN TRANSMISSION RELAYED TO HIGHCOM BRAVO SIX-OVER.
REQUEST SITREP- OVER.
ROGER-ABOARD FORERUNNER VESSEL.
DESTINATION EARTH-MINIMUM ONE PROPHET HIERARCH ON BOARD.
NO ESTIMATE FOR REMAINING CREW-
ROGER.
MORE TO FOLLOW.
FA-CHOOM

RUN!!
RUN!!!
DO YOU THINK HE SAW US??
THE DRAGON?? I DON'T KNOW. I DON'T SEE IT.
OH MY GOD!! HERE IT COMES!!
OH MAN!!
YOU HAVE TO TAKE IT, RUWAN!!! IT'S UP TO YOU NOW.
ME??
RUWAN, TAKE THE KEY OF OSANALAN TO THE CASTLE IN THE NORTH HILLS!!

NO, NO THE WIZARD SAID IT WAS YOUR TASK, JAMES!
BUT I HAVE TO FIGHT THE DRAGON.
NO, YOU GET THE KEY, I FIGHT THE DRAGON.
I'M OLDER, I FIGHT THE DRAGON.
I DON'T WANT TO TAKE THE KEY.
YOU HAVE TO.
COME ON!!
YOU GET TO KISS THE PRINCESS WHEN WE UNLOCK HER FROM HER PRISON.
I DON'T WANT TO KISS HER!! I WANT TO KISS THE DRAGON.
YOU WANT TO KISS THE DRAGON??
I WANT TO KILL THE DRAGON.
YOU SAID KISS.
I MEANT KILL!!
DRAGON KISSER.
I SAID KILL!!
TAKE THE KEY.
I WILL BATTLE THE DRAGON AND THEN YOU CAN KISS THE PRINCESS AND THE DRAGON.
NO!!
YOU KILL THE NEXT DRAGON. PROMISE.
HAVE AT THEE, YOU FIRE-BREATHING ASSFACE!!

RUWAN?
I FEEL LIKE I'M GOING INSANE...
I DON'T UNDERSTAND.
THE ALIEN A$$#*#%$. THEY SAID--THEY SAID THEY WANTED THE KEY OF OSANALAN.
YEAH?
RIGHT?
I--
YOU HEARD THEM, RIGHT?
YEAH, I GUESS...
I--
I MADE IT UP.
I DON'T UNDERSTAND.
MY BROTHER AND ME. WE MADE IT UP.
IT--IT WAS A GAME WE USED TO PLAY. WE WERE INTO TOLKIEN. WE WERE FANTASY NERDS.
WELL, HE WAS. HE WAS OLDER THAN ME AND I JUST DID WHATEVER HE DID.
WE MADE UP THIS--THIS WHOLE STORY. CHARACTERS, THINGS...
WE WERE TWO KNIGHTS. AND WE WERE ALWAYS LOOKING FOR THE KEY OF OSANALAN. BECAUSE IT HELD THE SECRET OF THE MAGIC GARDEN WHERE THIS PRINCESS...
WHAT THE @#$% ARE YOU **BABBLING** ABOUT??

THE KEY. THIS THING THEY WANT. THESE ALIENS...
I MADE IT UP WHEN I WAS A BOY. IT DOESN'T EXIST.
MAYBE IT DOES AND YOU DIDN'T KNOW IT.
(I WISH WE HAD A WAY TO CALL OUT.)
OSANALAN.
YEAH?
OSANALAN!
IT--IT'S NOT A COMMON WORD.
MAYBE WE HEARD IT WRONG.
I HEARD IT. HE SAID IT FOUR TIMES.
OKAY, WELL, WHERE'S YOUR BROTHER?
HE'S UNSC. I HONESTLY HAVE NO DAMN IDEA WHERE HE IS.
UP THERE SOMEWHERE...
YOUR BROTHER'S A SOLDIER AND YOU'RE A HOTEL CLERK?
CONCIERGE.
AND MY BROTHER'S NOT A SOLDIER. HE'S SPECIAL FORCES.
(WHATEVER THAT MEANS.)
HE'S SOME DEEP UNDERCOVER THING. I DON'T EVEN KNOW WHAT.
AND NO...WE DON'T TALK MUCH.
MAYBE--
WHAT?

MAYBE HE TOLD THEM ABOUT IT.
MY BROTHER TOLD THE COVENANT ALIENS ABOUT A MAKE BELIEVE KEY?
WHY?
I DON'T KNOW.
LET'S GO.
WHERE?
WE'RE GOING TO FIND MY BROTHER.
I THOUGHT YOU SAID HE--
READY.
WE'RE GOING OUT THERE??
WE CAN'T STAY HERE.
WHERE EXACTLY OUT THERE ARE WE GOING?
JUST SHOOT AT ANYTHING THAT ISN'T HUMAN.
SHOOT?
LOOK AT MISTER TOUGH GUY ALL OF A SUDDEN.
YEAH, LOOK AT ME.
VRRRROOOMMMMM

Aboard Forerunner Dreadnought
COMMANDER LEPIDUS, ARE WE TO BELIEVE THE DEMON IS STILL ABOARD THIS SHIP, ALIVE AND WELL?
YOUR EMINENCE, PLEASE ACCEPT MY MOST HUMBLEST APOLOGIES.
THE COUNCIL DEMANDS AN IMMEDIATE EXPLANATION.
YES, HOLY ONE. WE ARE FIXING THE SITUATION.
SIERRA ONE ONE SEVEN...
RADIO SILENCE.
BLAZZAAMM
BLAZZAAMM
BLAZZAAMM
BLAZZAAMM
SPLASH

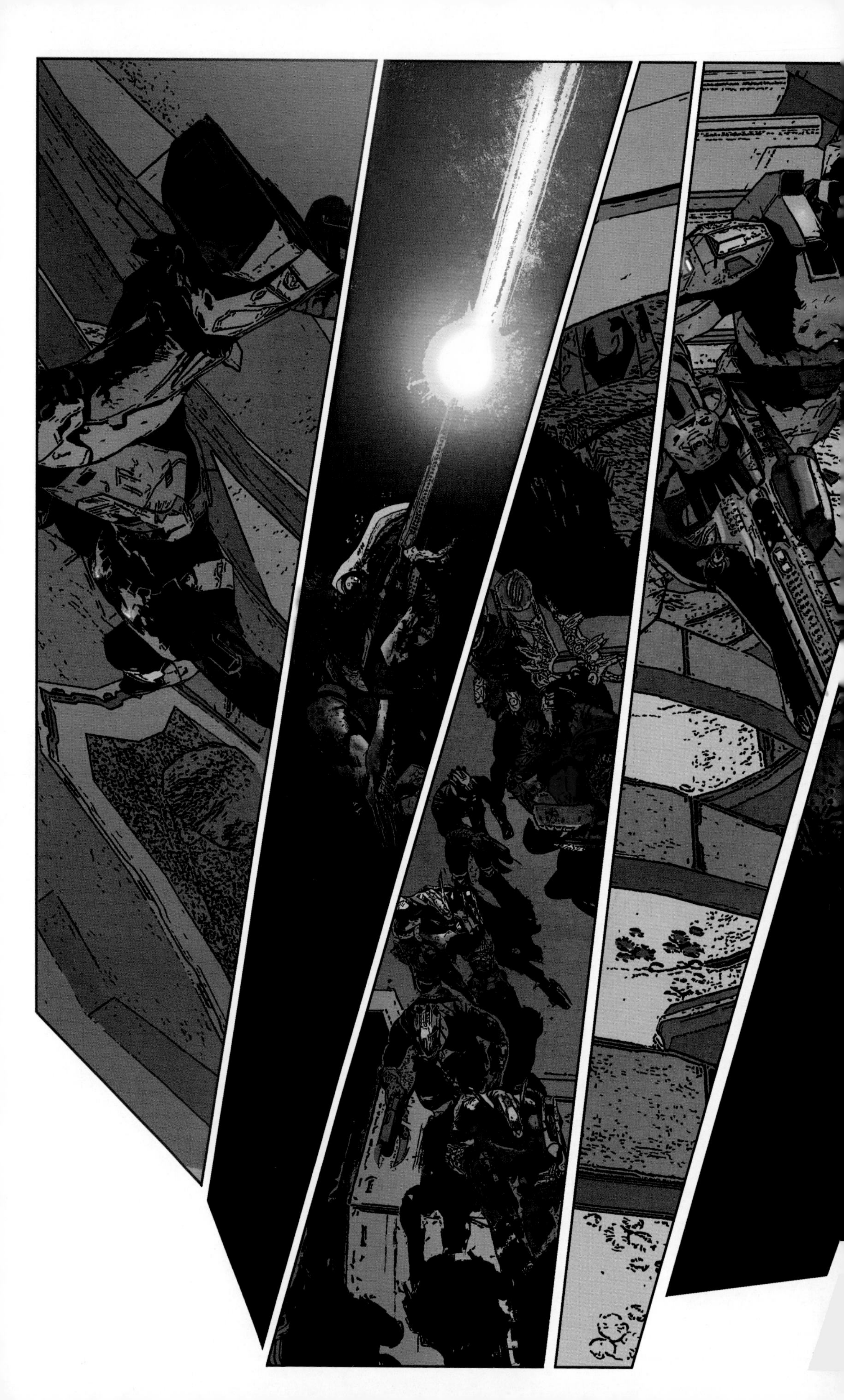

FFSSAAAAMM
PROTECT THE PROPHET!!
PROTECT THE PROPHET!!
FFSSAAAMM
FABOOM
FABOOM
FABOOM
FABOOM
FABOOM

FFSSAAAMM
FFSSAAAMM
FFSSAAAMM
FFSSAAAMM
FFSSAAAMM
FFSSAAAMM
FFSSAAAMM
FFSSAAAMM
FFSSAAAMM
FFSSAAAMM
SPASH
SPASH
SPASH
FFSSAAAMM
FFSSAAAMM
FFSSAAAMM
FFSSAAAMM
FFSSAAAMM
FFSSAAAMM
SPASH
SPASH
SPASH

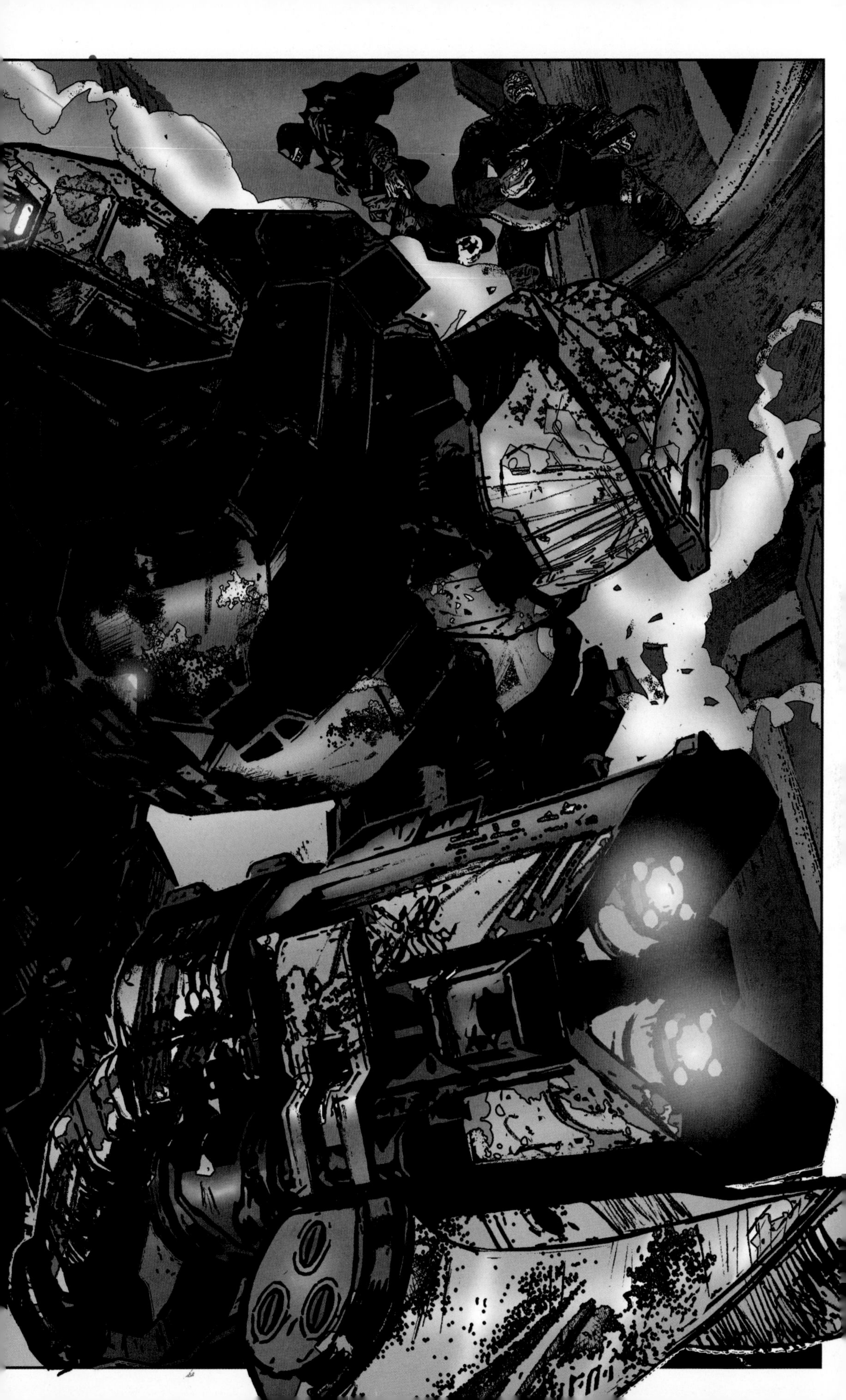

DO YOU KNOW WHERE YOU ARE?
(KIND OF.)
BUT LET'S JUST TRY TO STAY AWAY FROM THINGS THAT LOOK LIKE THAT!
ERT
AAAAGGHH!!
SHIT!!
SHIT!!
BUDDA BUDDA BUDDA BUDDA BUDDA BUDDA
SCREEEEEEEEEEEEE

FABOOM

AIE!
THUMP

SCREEEEEEVRRROOOMMM

NEVER THOUGHT I'D DO ANYTHING LIKE THAT.
NOTHING!!
WHAT??!!

HOLD IT TOGETHER.
WE'RE LOOKING-- ACTUALLY, WE'RE LOOKING FOR SOMETHING JUST LIKE THAT.
WHOAH! IS THAT OUR GUYS? IS THAT FOR US?
CAN THEY GET US THE #$% OUT OF HERE?
I THINK SO.

I THINK--I THINK IT'S A TRANSPORT.
OH THANK GOD!!
HEY, HEY!!!
DOES ANYONE KNOW COLONEL JAMES ACKERSON??!
GET IN THE TRANSPORT!!
COLONEL JAMES ACKERSON!!! IS HE HERE??
I'M WITH HIM!
MA'AM, WE'RE ON A TIME SITUATION--
I DON'T KNOW WHO YOU'RE TALKING ABOUT.
ACKERSON!!
COLONEL JAMES ACKERSON!!
ACKERSON?
I KNOW THAT GUY.
OH @#$%!
INCOMING!!
INCOMING!!

ARE YOU OKAY?
NO.
NO, I'M NOT.
ARE YOU?
YEAH, SURE...
MY--MY MOTTO USED TO BE...IF YOU'RE FEELING SHITTY ABOUT YOURSELF...
JUST IMAGINE THERE IS SOMEONE IN THE WORLD IN A WORSE SITUATION THAN YOU...

"...I'M JUST--I'M HAVING TROUBLE IMAGINING THAT RIGHT NOW."
FFSSAAMM
FFSSAAMM
FFSSAAMM

FFSAAAMM
FFSAAAMM
FFSAAAMM
FFSAAAMM
FFSAAAMM
FFSAAAMM
FFSAAAMM
FFSAAAMM

BBZZAATTZZ
BBZZAATTZZ
BBZZAATTZZ
BBZZAATTZZ
AGH!
SMASH

BBZZAATTZZ
BBZZAATTZZ
BBZZAATTZZ
BBZZAATTZZ
BBZZAATTZZ

THWAMM!

BBZZAATTZZ
BBZZAATTZZ
BBZZAATTZZ
AAGGHH!!

UNSC
ARE YOU OKAY SWEETY? DO YOU KNOW WHERE YOUR MOMMY IS?
THIS IS YOU, RIGHT? I REALLY LIKE YOUR MUSIC.
OH SWEETY, THAT'S NICE.
YOU LOOKING FOR ACKERSON?

HE'S ON MARS!
OR AT LEAST HE WAS WHEN THE COVENANT ATTACKED!!
YEAH.
CAN YOU GET ME IN TOUCH WITH HIM?!
I DON'T THINK SO!!
PLEASE!! I THINK-- IT'S IMPORTANT. HE'S MY BROTHER.
WE LOST MARS!!
YOU LOST..?
SORRY!!
MAYBE--MAYBE WE SHOULD TRY ANYHOW.

IF THE COVENANT ARE HERE, THAT MEANS UNSC MARS IS WIPED OUT!
I'M SORRY.

OR--OR MAYBE THEY **CAPTURED** HIM, RIGHT?
LIKE A PRISONER.

AGAIN, I DON'T MEAN TO BE MEAN...
BUT IF THAT'S THE CASE...LET'S **HOPE** HE'S DEAD.
HERE'S THE THING. AND PLEASE, YOU HAVE TO LISTEN!!
THIS KEY. THIS KEY THAT THE COVENANT ARE LOOKING FOR HERE...
YEAH, I DON'T KNOW ANYTHING ABOUT THAT. ALIEN @#$HEADS ALWAYS LOOKING FOR SOME--
I DO.
ME AND MY BROTHER. THAT WAS A THING FROM WHEN WE WERE KIDS.
I DON'T UNDERSTAND!!
WE **MADE IT UP** WHEN WE WERE KIDS.
IT WAS A GAME OF KNIGHTS AND DRAGONS AND WE WERE LOOKING FOR THIS KEY.
THIS KEY WAS A GAME!! IT'S NOT REAL!
YOU GOTTA BE **SHITTING ME!!?**
THE KEY!! IT'S SO SPECIFIC. THE NAME!!
THE **ONLY** PEOPLE WHO KNEW THAT NAME WERE **ME** AND **MY BROTHER.**
AND IF YOU KNOW MY BROTHER, YOU KNOW WHAT HIS UNSC STATUS IS. YOU SEE?
I THINK HIS BROTHER TOLD THEM ABOUT A "KEY" SO THEY WOULDN'T DESTROY **THIS** CITY--

I THINK HE DID IT TO TRY AND SAVE HIS BROTHER'S LIFE AND MAYBE GIVE YOU GUYS AN ANGLE TO STOP THE MADNESS.
SEE? THEY AREN'T DESTROYING **THIS** CITY. NOT LIKE THE OTHERS. NOT LIKE MOMBASA.

HEY, YOU'RE FAMOUS.
PLEASE FOCUS.
I TOLD YOU-- ME AND MY BROTHER AREN'T EVEN SPEAKING REALLY.
YEAH, WELL, WHAT ELSE MAKES SENSE??
SITE SEVEN, THIS IS BLUE LEADER...
PATCH ME THROUGH TO COMMAND!

I'VE GOT SOMEBODY HERE I THINK THEY SHOULD TALK TO.

KCHUNK
KCHUNK
KCHUNK
SPANG

Cleveland Sewers
UM.
UM, I JUST WANTED TO KNOW...
RITCHIE AND CALINACK, FALL BACK. MAKE SURE WE GOT IN CLEAN.
YES, SIR!
DON'T TOUCH AN ARMED UNSC SOLDIER, SIR.
SORRY, I JUST-
NEVER TOUCH US. GOOD WAY TO LOSE A BODY PART.
I WAS JUST WONDERING--
WE'RE ALMOST THERE.
I WAS JUST WONDERING WHERE EXACTLY WE ALMOST--?
WE'RE UNDER THE CITY, RIGHT? THIS IS THE OLD SEWERS?
ARE WE UNDER THE CITY?
JUST HOLD IT TOGETHER, KID, AND WE'LL GET YOU ALL SETTLED IN.
KID?
NOW, KID, LISTEN TO ME CAREFULLY...
(I'M NOT A KID.)
SEE HIM? THAT'S THE MAN.
THE MAN IN CHARGE. SERGEANT TWYKER.
EVERYTHING YOU TOLD ME, YOU TELL HIM.

WHAT'S THIS NOW?
SERGEANT TWYKER. THIS IS A REFUGEE FROM THE CITY PROPER. AND THIS IS HIS--
AND WHAT THE HELL THEY DOIN' DOWN HERE, SOLDIER?!!
TELL HIM.
MY--MY NAME IS RUWAN. I'M A CONCIERGE AT THE HOTEL...
I DON'T CARE.
THE--THE KEY THE ALIENS ARE LOOKING FOR. THEY SAID THEY'RE LOOKING FOR A KEY.
YEAH?!
I DON'T GIVE TWO FLYING--
LET HIM TALK, SIR.
I'M WESLEY. INTEL OPERATIONS MANAGER.
YOU KNOW WHAT I'M TALKING ABOUT?
YEAH, THEY'RE TEARING UP THE CITY LOOKING FOR A KEY OF--ERR...
OF OSANALAN.
YEAH.
IT DOESN'T EXIST.
IT DOESN'T? AND HOW WOULD YOU KNOW SOMETHING LIKE--?
I MADE IT UP.

YOU MADE IT UP?
I DID. ME AND MY BROTH--
GET HIM OUT OF HERE!! WHAT ARE YOU-- SOLDIER?
ARE YOU A ROOK? THE GUY'S OFF THE STREET YOU BRING HIM INTO A SECURE MARINE HQ?!
NO, SIR, I--
NO, NO. MY BROTHER IS SPECIAL FORCES. HE'S--
NO SHIT.
YEAH...
YOUR BROTHER OWES ME MONEY FROM WAY BACK.
YEAH, THAT SOUNDS LIKE HIM.
AND I THINK THE ALIENS CAPTURED HIS BROTHER. AND HE TOLD THEM ABOUT THIS "KEY" TO--TO SCREW WITH THEM.
TO--TO GET THEM TO GO OFF THEIR PLANS.
TO SPARE THIS CITY! TO SAVE HIS BROTHER!
I THINK HE SENT THEM HERE LOOKING FOR SOMETHING THAT DOESN'T EXIST TO GIVE YOU GUYS A FIGHTING CHANCE.
I WANT A SCAN OF THIS GUY. I WANT PROOF OF IDENTIFICATION
IT'S GOOD. HE READS CLEAN.
DOES ANY OF THIS HELP YOU AT ALL?

TELL HIM WHO YOUR BROTHER IS!
ACKERSON.
COLONEL JAMES ACKERSON.
NO, THAT'S-- YEAH...
AND YOU MADE IT UP? THE KEY?
AS KIDS. THIS IS--THIS IS WHAT I'M SAYING.
HEY, YOU LOOK FAMILIAR.
THERE **IS** NO KEY?
THERE--**IS** NO KEY.
LET'S GET A KEY, WRAP IT IN TIN FOIL, GIVE IT TO THE BASTARDS, AND SEND THEM ON THEIR WAY.
NO NO NO...
WE CAN--
YOU KNOW **WHAT?** WE CAN DO **A LOT** BETTER THAN THAT.
LIKE WHAT?

Covenant Fleet, High Earth Orbit
THIS IS SIERRA ONE ONE SEVEN. OVER.
WE READ YOU, SIERRA ONE ONE SEVEN, LOCATION AND SITUATION. OVER?
I SECURED THE BRIDGE OF THE FORERUNNER VESSEL.
I AM IN LOW EARTH ORBIT.
THERE IS A COVENANT PROPHET ON BOARD BUT HIS LOCATION IS UNKNOWN.
I AM SURROUNDED BY AN ARMADA OF COVENANT VESSELS IN OR AROUND EARTH'S ORBIT.
THE COVENANT IS AWARE OF MY PRESENCE AND IS PREPARING TO ENGAGE.
STAND BY FOR ORDERS. OVER.

Forerunner
Dreadnought
STANDING BY. OVER.
FFSSAAMM
FFSSAAMM
FBOOOMMM

FABOOMMM
SIERRA ONE ONE SEVEN, WHAT WAS THAT? OVER.
HOLDING POSITION. OVER.
STAND BY.
PROCEED TO BRIDGE, NEW COORDINATES INCOMING.

Chagrin Falls, Ohio
THE SEVEN YEAR ITCH
JUNE 6
JUNE 20
JULY 11
JULY 25
DID YOU HEAR ME?
WHAT?
I SAID: HERE'S WHAT'S GOING TO HAPPEN...

THROUGH CHANNELS, CONTACT IS BEING MADE WITH COVENANT FORCES.
WE'RE TELLING THEM WE HAVE THE KEY. WE'RE OFFERING A NEUTRAL DROP-OFF POINT.
IT'LL TAKE SOME TIME BUT IF THEY BITE--IF WE GET WORD BACK...MOST PROBABLY THEY'LL PICK THE LOCATION. THEN WE SEND IN ONE OF OUR MEN-
I'LL DO IT.
DO WHAT?
THE DROP-OFF.
(OR WHATEVER YOU CALL IT.)
NO. WE HAVE MEN FOR THIS.
BUT--
WE GOT IT.
NO. NO. I WANT TO DO IT. I SHOULD DO IT. IT'S MY FAULT.
YOUR FAULT?
I BROUGHT THIS TO YOU. I BROUGHT THIS TO YOU.
IF THEY ASK ANY QUESTIONS ABOUT IT--ANY OTHER CHILDHOOD BS MY BROTHER MIGHT HAVE TOLD THEM--WHO'S MORE LIKELY TO KNOW? ME OR SOME RANDOM MARINE? I MIGHT BE ABLE TO BUY SOME MORE TIME...
RIGHT?
THEY'LL JUST THINK IT'S A TRAP OR A SOMETHING--
REALLY? I HAVE TO DO IT.
HE HAS A POINT. ALL OUR INTEL IS BASED ON HIS BROTHER'S BS AND TO BE HONEST, WE NEED EVERY FIGHTING MAN WE CAN SPARE.
I NEED EVERY MAN WITH A WEAPON I GOT.
SIR, ALL DUE RESPECT, YOU DON'T GIVE A CLASSIFIED COVERT OP TO A CIVILIAN IN THE TIME OF--
THIS AIN'T A COVERT OP.
YOU KNOW WHAT THIS IS...

IT'S A DAMNED DIRTY POOL PISS IN THE WIND.
DIRTY POOL?
IT'S WHAT MY GRANDPA USED TO CALL IT.
WE'RE LOSING THE WAR. WE'RE LOSING GROUND AS WE SPEAK. THIS IS A DIRTY LITTLE TRICK TO GET SOME BACK.
HEY, I'M NOT SHITTING ON IT. WE TAKE ANY ANGLE WE CAN GET.
YOU'RE REALLY GOING?
UM, IF THEY LET ME.
IS THIS THE SAME GUY WHO I MET HIDING UNDER HIS DESK YESTERDAY?
YEAH. HOW ABOUT THAT?
I CAN GET US OUT OF HERE. SOME OF THESE GUYS KNOW MY MUSIC.
FAMOUS PEOPLE CAN GET A LIFT OUT OF **ANYWHERE.**
I HEARD BEING FAMOUS IS COOL LIKE **THAT.**
IT IS.
SO HOW ABOUT WE DO **THAT?** HOW ABOUT YOU COME **WITH** ME?
I--
I THINK I HAVE TO DO **THIS.**
WHAT IF YOUR BROTHER WAS TRYING TO **SAVE** YOU FROM ALL THIS?

MAYBE HE WAS.
BUT--BUT I THINK I HAVE TO DO THIS ANYWAY.
OK, WELL, WHAT IF I'M BEING SELFISH AND I WANT YOU TO NOT DO THIS BECAUSE I'M REALLY...
...GLAD WE MET.
REALLY?
YEAH, HOW ABOUT THAT?
REALLY?
YES. SO...
SO, MAY THAT BE YOUR INCENTIVE FOR YOU--FOR BOTH OF US TO GET OUT OF ALL THIS ALIVE.
WELL, THAT'S-- UH--THAT'S A PRETTY GOOD INCENTIVE.
I'M ALIVE BECAUSE OF YOU.

IT WAS **BOTH** OF US.
OK, MAYBE A LITTLE.
IT WAS.
HEY, WILL YOU, UM, WRITE A PIECE OF MUSIC ABOUT IT?
I GUARANTEE IT.
THAT'S SOMETHING.
THAT'S--THAT ALMOST MAKES ALL THIS WORTHWHILE.
COME BACK AND I'LL PLAY IT FOR YOU.
IT'S TIME.
THEY WANT TO MEET.
THEY WANT THE KEY.

HUMAN.
THE KEY.
HAND IT OVER.
UM, OK.
WHERE IS IT?
IT'S ME.
I'M THE KEY.

Dreadnought Bridge
KLAN KLANG KLANG
BOOM
BOOM
FASHOOM FASSSHHOOMMM
BOOM BOOM
FASHOOM FASSSHHOOMMM
TURN THE SHIP. HARD LEFT, FORTY DEGREES. NOW.
FSHAAMMM
SIERRA ONE ONE SEVEN...FORERUNNER VESSEL IS ON A FIXED COURSE. FLIGHT PATH CANNOT BE ALTERED, OVER.
UNDERSTOOD. WE WILL GO TO PLAN B TO TAKE OUT THE TARGET. OVER.

COMMANDER, IS THE UNHOLY ONE STILL ON BOARD?
Prophet Of Truth's Quarters
WE'RE TAKING BACK CONTROL OF THE BRIDGE.
THE SPARTAN IS NOT HERE.
THERE'S NO SIGN OF HIM.
IT'S BEST WE GET YOU OFF THIS SHIP, HOLY ONE.
I WANT THIS SITUATION TAKEN CARE OF. IT IS ONLY ONE HUMAN.
ONE HUMAN!!
YOUR EXCELLENCE, WORD FROM FLIGHT DECK...
HE'S COMMANDEERED A GHOST. HE'S HEADED OUT THE AIR LOCK.
ILLUMINATE HIM.

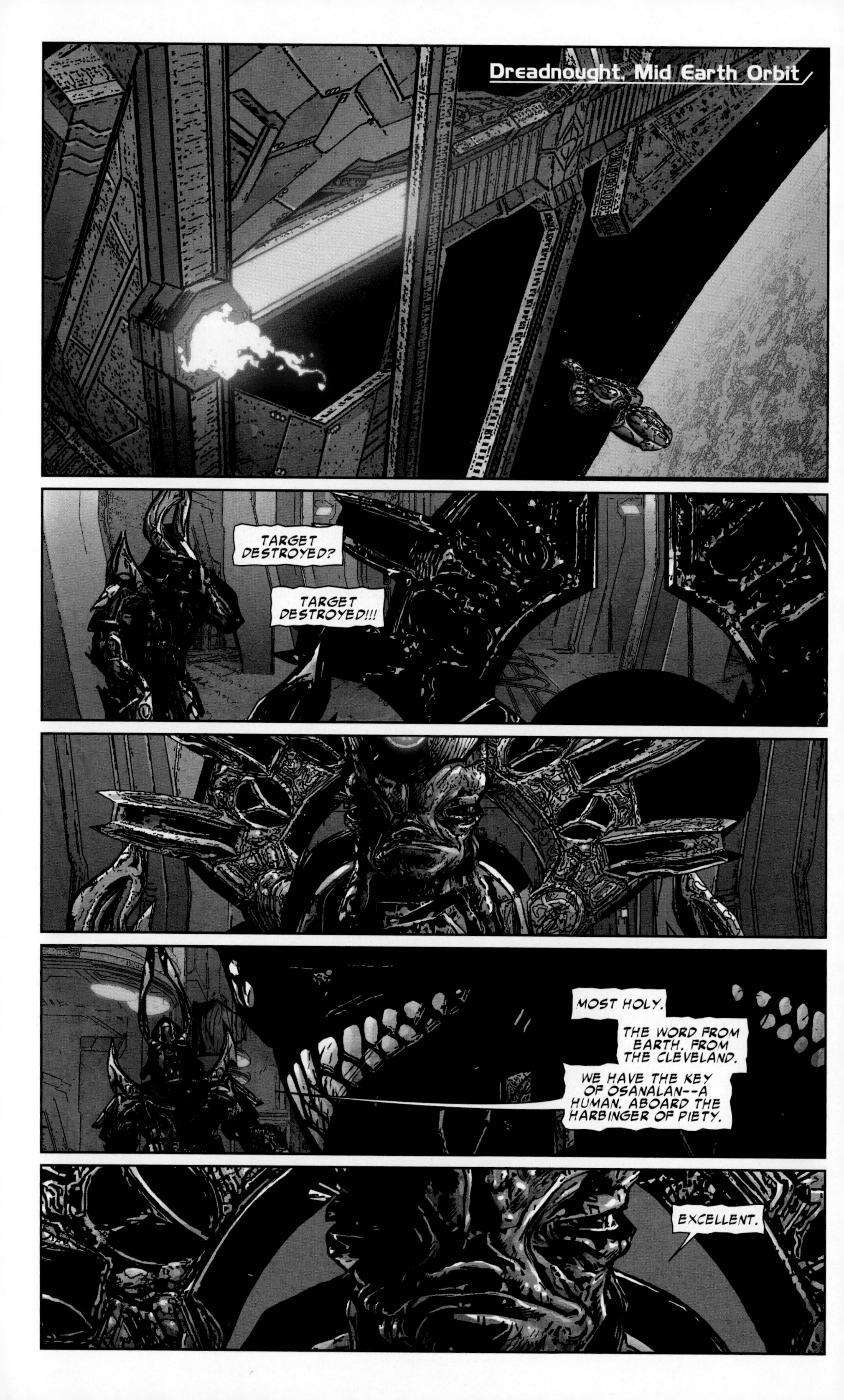
Dreadnought, Mid Earth Orbit
TARGET DESTROYED?
TARGET DESTROYED!!!
MOST HOLY.
THE WORD FROM EARTH. FROM THE CLEVELAND.
WE HAVE THE KEY OF OSANALAN--A HUMAN. ABOARD THE HARBINGER OF PIETY.
EXCELLENT.

OK MISTER. YOU WANT TO BE THE HERO?
HERE'S HOW YOU'LL BE THE HERO.
WE'RE INJECTING YOU WITH TYKOS 30.
IT'S AN ORGANIC TRACKING MATERIAL. LOOKS A LOT LIKE BLOOD PLASMA.
NON-METALLIC. NON-PLASTIC.
WE CAN TRACK YA TO MARS IF THAT'S WHERE THE COVENANT TAKE YA.
WE CAN TRACK YOU. THEY CAN'T.
ORGANIC MATERIAL?
IF WE GIVE YA A GUN OR SHOVE A GRENADE UP YOUR HOO HAH, THEN THEY'LL MELT YOUR HEAD BEFORE YOU SAY HI.
BUT THIS STUFF? THEY DON'T KNOW ABOUT IT AND THEY WON'T BE ABLE TO TRACK IT.
THEY'LL THINK YOU'RE UNARMED. AND YOU WILL BE.
SEE, THESE BRUTES. LET ME TELL YA...
TACTICAL VIE

AT THIS LEVEL, THEY'RE DUMB. WORKER BEES WITH GUNS AND ARMOR.
THE SECOND YOU HIT 'EM WITH SOMETHING THEY DON'T UNDERSTAND THEY PANIC AND RUN TO COMMAND.
YOU'LL SAY THAT YOU'RE THE KEY... THEY'LL RUN TO MOMMY.
BUTCHERY
THEY MAY SAY SCREW IT AND NOT CALL US BACK.
THEY MAY SAY SCREW IT AND TAKE YOU TO A COMMAND CENTER AND TORTURE YOU FOR INTEL...
TRY TO GET YOU TO SAY SOMETHIN' BUT YOU WON'T BECAUSE YOU DON'T KNOW ANYTHING.
EVEN IF YOU TELL THEM WHERE WE ARE, WE'LL BE GONE BEFORE YOU CAN EVEN--

THEY'LL PANIC. CALL UP TO COVENANT COMMAND.
COMMAND WILL SAY IT'S A TRICK. HE'S ARMED.
THEY'LL ASSURE COMMAND THAT YOU ARE NOT.
THEN COMMAND WILL GO TO THEIR SUPERIORS.
THE HOPE IS THAT THEY WILL BE SO OVERWHELMED WITH RELIGIOUS, I DON'T KNOW, FERVOR AND CURIOSITY THEY WILL NEED TO SEE YOU FOR THEMSELVES.
THEY WILL NEED TO QUESTION YOU THEMSELVES.
THEY MAY ASK TO HAVE YOU TAKEN RIGHT TO SOME SECRET LOCATION.
I WOULD NEVER DO THAT.

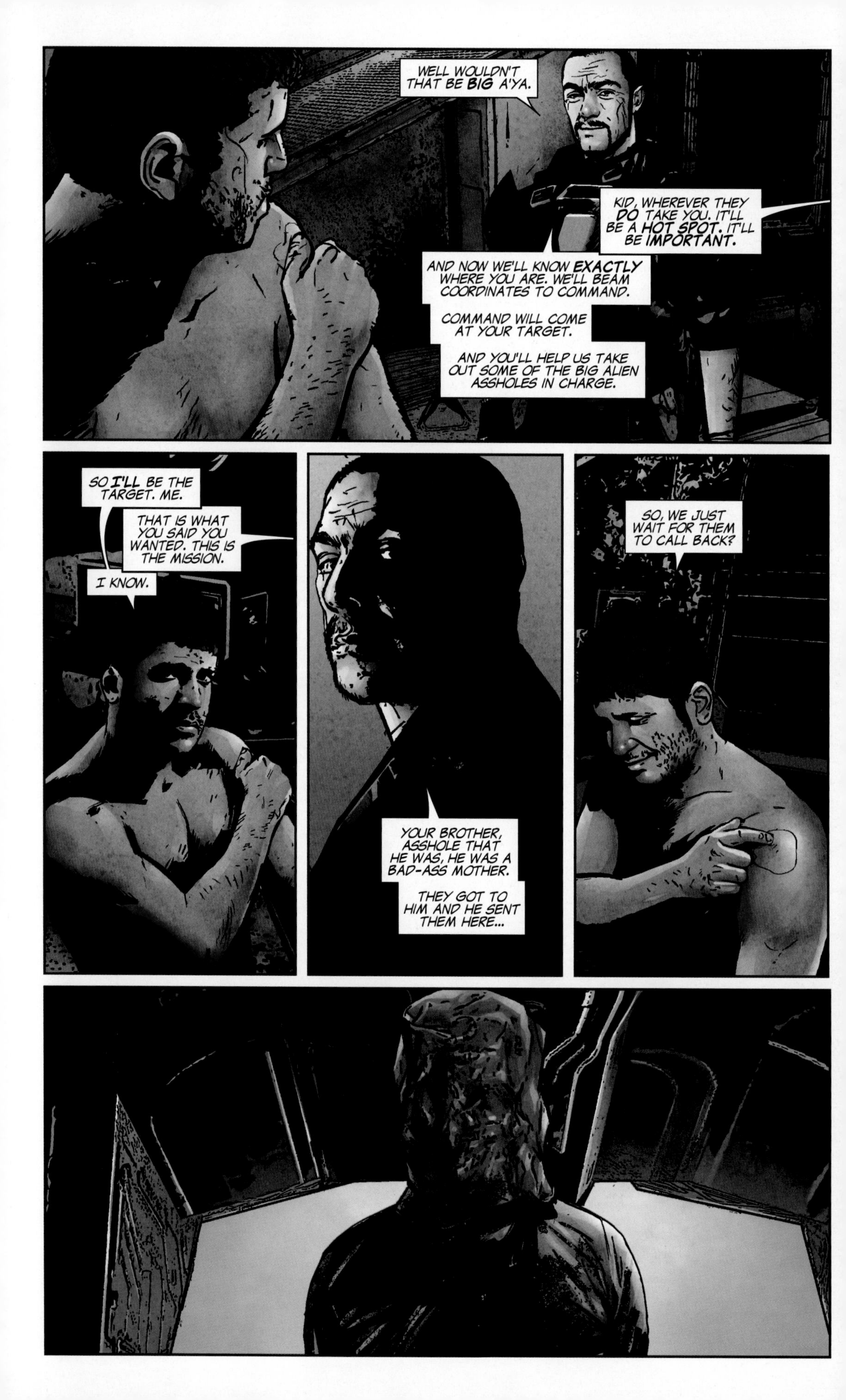
WELL WOULDN'T THAT BE BIG A'YA.
KID, WHEREVER THEY DO TAKE YOU. IT'LL BE A HOT SPOT. IT'LL BE IMPORTANT.
AND NOW WE'LL KNOW EXACTLY WHERE YOU ARE. WE'LL BEAM COORDINATES TO COMMAND.
COMMAND WILL COME AT YOUR TARGET.
AND YOU'LL HELP US TAKE OUT SOME OF THE BIG ALIEN ASSHOLES IN CHARGE.
SO I'LL BE THE TARGET. ME.
THAT IS WHAT YOU SAID YOU WANTED. THIS IS THE MISSION.
I KNOW.
YOUR BROTHER, ASSHOLE THAT HE WAS, HE WAS A BAD-ASS MOTHER.
THEY GOT TO HIM AND HE SENT THEM HERE...
SO, WE JUST WAIT FOR THEM TO CALL BACK?

Covenant Cruiser
Harbinger Of Piety

AGH!

AGH...

Chamber of the Minister Of Inquisition,
Harbinger Of Piety
HUMAN...SO THIS IS THE KEY OF OSANALAN?
TELL US, CREATURE... WHAT DO YOU OPEN?
HALO?
THIS IS A LIVE HARD TARGET IN YOUR RADIUS. IMMEDIATE EVASIVE ACTION REQUIRED.
RECEIVED. OVER.

Y-YES.
THIS IS TWYKER ON CODED LINE NINER SEVEN. WE HAVE A LOCATION FOR THE KEY.
HE'S STOPPED MOVING. HE'S IN ORBIT. HE'S ON BOARD A SHIP.
COMMAND, WE'VE GOT A HARD LOCK TARGET.
WE'RE SENDING COORDINATES TO YOU, GAMMA NINE DELTA ONE. DO YOU READ? OVER.
SIERRA ONE ONE SEVEN, COORDINATES ARE BEING UPLOADED. OVER.
INTEL RECEIVED.
TELL US WHAT YOU KNOW OF THE HALO?
TELL ME WHAT YOU ARE AND I WILL SPARE YOUR INSIGNIFICANT PLANET.

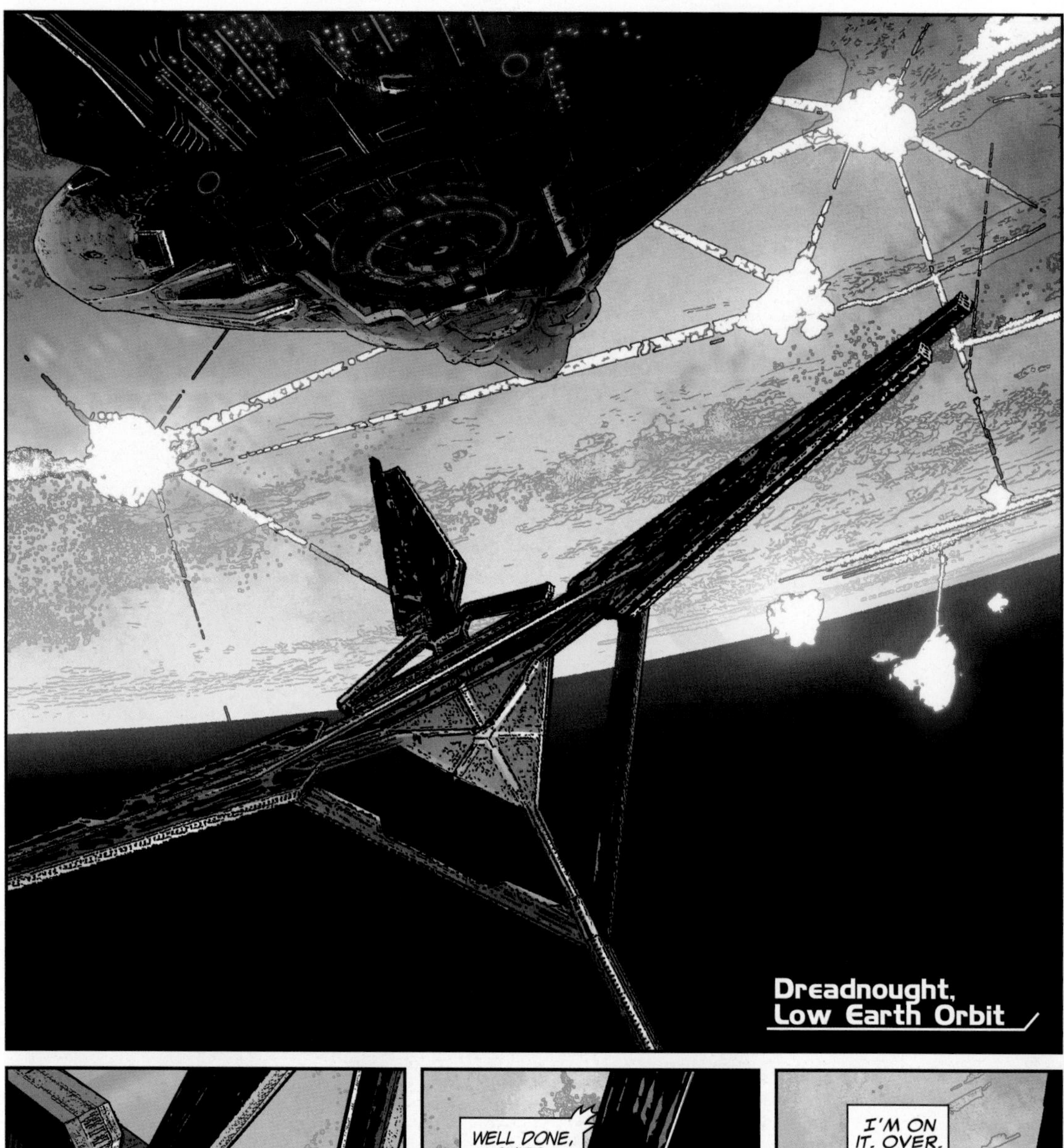
Dreadnought,
Low Earth Orbit

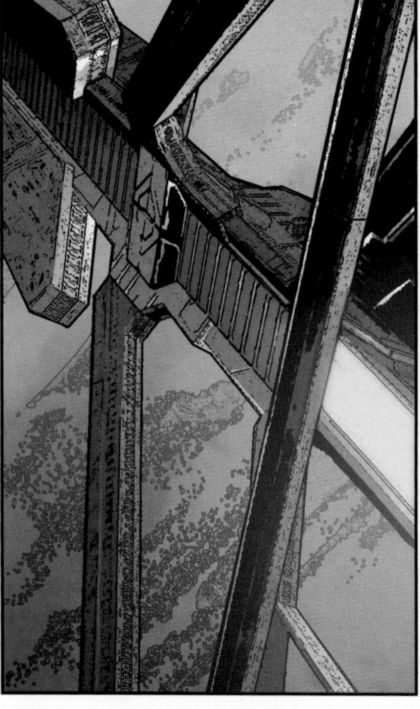

WELL DONE, CHIEF.
THE "KEY" IS ABOUT TO GET A SPECIAL DELIVERY. SUGGEST YOU FIND A QUICK WAY HOME.

I'M ON IT. OVER.

RUN!!
RUN!!!

DID YOU THINK WE WERE UNAWARE OF THE TRACKING DEVICE YOU WEAR? DID YOU THINK YOUR FRIENDS WOULD COME TO RESCUE YOU? THIS SHIP IS IMPREGNABLE. IT HAS LAID WASTE TO WORLDS. LET THEM COME. WE WELCOME THEM.
IT'S NOT A RESCUE SIGNAL.
THEN, PRAY TE WHAT IS IT?
IT'S A TARGETING VECTOR. I'M THE TARGET.
Nassau Station
MAC Platform

WHAT?
KISS MY ASS.

Mars Orbit
HUMAN!!
THERE IS NO KEY OF OSANALAN, IS THERE?!
ACKERSON!!
ARE YOU ASKING A QUESTION OR STATING A FACT??
THERE IS NO KEY?!!
HAHAHAHAHAHAHAHA!!
YEAH, THAT WAS A GOOD ONE. EVEN FOR ME.
WHOO!!
I GOTTA KNOW... HOW MUCH OF YOUR EARTH CAMPAIGN DID YOU LOSE TRYING TO FIND IT?
COME ON, I REALLY WANT TO KNOW...
HOW MANY OF YOU IDIOTS DID IT TAKE TO SCREW IN AN IMAGINARY LIGHTBULB?
SEE, THAT'S WHY YOU'RE GOING TO LOSE.
ALL YOUR POMP AND THINKING YOU'RE SO RIGHT ABOUT EVERYTHING...
WHEN IT COMES DOWN TO IT YOU'RE JUST DUMB AND ARROGANT AND--
THAT'S WHY WE'LL WIN.

UNSC Relief Camp,
Akron, Ohio

WAIT FOR ME!
KISS MY ASS!

INSIDE *HALO: UPRISING*
AND MORE WITH
BRIAN MICHAEL BENDIS,
ALEX MALEEV, BRIAN JARRARD
AND FRANK O'CONNOR

PLUGGING IN T

Halo is more than just a video game, it's a multi-media experience that has taken hold of the imagination of millions in only a few short years. Marvel is proud to present *Halo: Uprising*, a high-concept, four-issue limited series that links the narrative of the *Halo 2* and *Halo 3* games. *Marvel Spotlight* is proud to take readers and gamers inside the melding of two simpatico artforms!

I: The Halo Effect: An Interview With Brian Michael Bendis

It's always a blast when *Spotlight* gets to talk with writer Brian Michael Bendis, but things get really explosive when the Master Chief is on the list of topics! *Halo: Uprising* may only seem to take Bendis out of his element as one of Marvel's grittiest, street-level, super hero scribes, but he's here to explain how that's not the case!

II: The Halo Effect: An Interview With Alex Maleev

Artist Alex Maleev already has made history with Bendis in a *Daredevil* run that not only defied expectations but also created all new ones for other creators to follow! *Spotlight* takes a look at *DD*, his other collaborations with Bendis, and his love for the *Halo* game that has inspired the new comic he is working on!

III: Waiting For the Flood:
Halo Nation Comes to Marvel

Halo veterans Brian Jarrard and Frank O'Connor are on hand to take comic readers inside the world of Halo and to discuss the making of Halo 3, Halo comics, and the rest of the huge Halo universe!

Please Note: These interviews took place in 2007 prior to the release of *Halo Uprising #1*.

CREDITS:

Head Writer/Coordinator:
John Rhett Thomas

Spotlight Bullpen Writer:
Dugan Trodglen

Layout:
BLAMMO! Content & Design, Rommel & Regina Alama

THE HALO EFFECT

AN INTERVIEW WITH WRITER

AS CREATIVE TEAMS GO, *HALO: UPRISING* COULDN'T HAVE HAD A BETTE
FARE, AS WRITER BRIAN MICHAEL BENDIS AND ARTIST ALEX MALEEV H

BRIAN MICHAEL BENDIS

TO LAUNCH THE VIDEO GAME'S ENTRY INTO MONTHLY MARVEL COMICS
ITE THE TRACK RECORD OF SUCCESS BEHIND THEM. BY DUGAN TRODGLEN

HALOS AND HAND GRENADES:
Meet the Master Chief, the only thing standing between the Covenant and you!

Writer Brian Michael Bendis.

IT'S PRETTY SAFE TO SAY THAT BRIAN MICHAEL BENDIS IS THE MOST INFLUENTIAL COMIC BOOK WRITER OF THE LAST TEN YEARS, AND CERTAINLY THE MOST IMPORTANT CREATIVE FORCE AT MARVEL COMICS DURING THAT TIME.

He joined the House of Ideas in 2000 to launch the landmark *Ultimate Spider-Man* series, which he's still writing over 100 issues later (with no end in sight), and on the back of which the entire Ultimate line has its foundation. In 2004 he took over *The Avengers* with a plan to dismantle them in *Disassembled*, the shocking event in which the team was destroyed from within. From the ashes of that storyline came the eminently successful *New Avengers*, part of a cascading series of events that put the Avengers family of titles on a road that would lead to them actually overtaking the X-Men books as Marvel's premiere line, culminating in the smash limited series *House of M* (written by Bendis) and *Civil War.* • Many people say, however, that the Marvel book Brian will most be remembered for is *Daredevil*. Along with his *Halo: Uprising* partner Alex Maleev, Brian was able to carve out a legend on a book already rich with legendary runs. Brian, who seems so at home with "street level" heroes and pulp crime stories, was a surprising choice to write a comic based on *Halo*, a hardcore sci-fi video game. But as will be revealed in the following interview, he turns out to be the perfect choice! *Spotlight* talked to Bendis about writing this high-profile project and about working with Alex Maleev on such a diverse group of comic books.

"THEY'VE GOT MOEBIUS; THEY DON'T CARE ABOUT BALD LITTLE ULTIMATE SPIDER-MAN BOY"
—WRITER MICHAEL BENDIS ON PITCHING FOR THE *HALO* JOB

SPOTLIGHT: So Brian, are you a video game fan yourself?

BRIAN: Oh, yeah. And a video game writer! Absolutely.

SPOTLIGHT: And *Halo* in particular?

BRIAN: Definitely. Alex and I were big fans. Alex is a master *Halo* player and any free time he has he plays *Halo*. He's much better than I am. But you write what you can't do!

SPOTLIGHT: *(Laughter)* So Alex was a master, huh? I guess that made him a great choice for the book.

BRIAN: Yeah, and he trusts me a lot. And I knew he would kill on this thing. He had inherently done all the hard work: he knew

RUWAN AND MYRAS: The two featured characters of *Halo: Uprising*.

BRIAN: I had a funny history with this project. This never really happens, but Marvel called me up and said, "Listen, we need you to do us a favor. Ruwan (Jayatilleke, VP of Development) is going up to Seattle and he's gonna try to close the *Halo* deal. We really want to do the *Halo Graphic Novel*. Can you go up there and be the pretty girl?" I was like, "What?!?!", and they said, "If you came up, maybe they could see how serious we are, and they'd be happy to meet you." So I went up there. I was surprised that they had already finished the graphic novel. I thought Marvel was trying to get the rights to make the GN, not publish one already completed. But it was already done, and Moebius had worked on it, and Simon Bisley. As soon as I saw the Moebius pages I thought, "They don't care if I'm here or not. They've got Moebius; they don't care about bald little *Ultimate Spider-Man* boy."

But it was a very nice meeting and I got to see first hand just how serious they were about it not sucking and how just because it's licensed and based on a product it doesn't have to suck. I was always boggled by how all of the highest profile comics – the tie-ins, the giveaways – have always been the lamest books. There had been a few books that had excelled past that. The *Blade Runner* and *Close Encounters* adaptations were exceptional. I always admired that. *Micronauts* is another example of taking something that could have ended up goofy and making it art. I remember thinking as I left that meeting, "Boy, if what they're saying is true, I'd love to get my hands on that one day." Because I do think that *Halo* is like this generation's *Star Wars* - at the beginning [of *Star Wars*], right before they merchandised the crap out of it. Here's this thing that has completely captured the world's imagination, but hasn't been licensed to death yet. To get in on the ground floor and tell some stories would be great.

SPOTLIGHT: And, of course, the *Halo* OGN came out and was a massive success.

BRIAN: Yeah, and soon after the graphic novel orders came in I knew there was already a plan for these series. And (Marvel Publisher) Dan Buckley or somebody approached me and said they really wanted Alex (to draw it). I said, "Wow. Well I'll do it, too, if you guys want." They said, "Yeah," and I guess they were kind of asking me in the first place! They also weren't sure if Alex would do it, because Alex is very serious about his comic art and what he'll apply it to. So I called Alex and said, "Hey, you wanna do *Halo* for a couple of months?" and he said "Really?!?" and I said, "Yeah, and I think we have a wide open playing field for what kind of story we can tell." So I pitched the story to Bungie and that went pretty smoothly and we were off and running.

SPOTLIGHT: And what is the story you've done?

BRIAN: They said they wanted the story to take place between (the video games) *Halo 2* and *3*. (We) asked if we could make the story the connecting tissue, starting at the end of 2 and ending at the beginning of 3. They said yes, so for Master Chief and Earth, it takes place at the end of *Halo 2*. For those who didn't finish *Halo 2* (like me – I had to go buy the DVD of the cinematics to see what happens, since I couldn't finish the game because I suck!) (*Laughter*), Master Chief is on the Forerunner, which is the big Covenant ship. The

CLEVELAND ROCKS: And it's also about to roll – under the terrifying invasion of the Covenant in *Halo: Uprising*.

Covenant are the aliens who are, you know, taking over, and who Master Chief has been fighting for the last two games. So they're headed toward Earth, and Master Chief has to do whatever he can to stop what's going on. So we're telling that story, but the meat of the story is what's happening on Earth, where there's already been an infiltration, and a full-scale invasion is coming.

What's cute is there are a lot of cities that are parts of *Halo* and the guys at *Halo* asked if I wanted to set this in Cleveland. That's where I was born, so I thought that was very sweet of them. I had just visited Cleveland recently for my brother's wedding and saw what a (mess) it had turned into. So I imagined, "Wouldn't it be nice to build a nice Cleveland on top of the (messy) Cleveland?" That's kind of what they did in the game with Mombasa, where there's an Old Mombasa and a New Mombasa.

So Alex and I developed a New Cleveland on top of the old. So New Cleveland is this new, beautiful, gleaming resort city that people pay to go to. People come from Paris to Cleveland for vacation! (*Laughter*). So we're doing what we can do in fantasy what can't ever be done in real life!

"I'VE BEEN SECRETLY WORKING IN HARDCORE SCI-FI FOR A WHILE!"

So a hunk of the story takes place in Cleveland, which is a beautiful resort city that's taking punishment from the Covenant and we meet a couple of new characters as they try to make heads or tails of the situation and try to survive what's happening. One of the characters has a connection to the armed forces that he is not aware of until later on in the story.

SPOTLIGHT: Are you introducing characters that will then be in *Halo 3*?

BRIAN: No, but it does get Master Chief from *Halo 2* to *Halo* 3. What we're able to do, which I'm very excited about, is, like the graphic novel did, flesh out what's taking place on Earth: what the human condition is, what people are feeling. In the game, we always see the military point of view - especially Master Chief's. We get either his or the Covenant's point of view, but we haven't really felt the human level perspective. The closest reference I have is the newest *War of the Worlds* that Spielberg did. We never left Tom Cruise's point of view. His narrow view of a larger story is where we stay. And here, we follow the "B" story: these two human characters who don't know each other who are running for their lives together as the world falls apart and not even knowing why.

SPOTLIGHT: Does it feel different writing about video game characters and that world? Did having written the script for the *Ultimate Spider-Man* video game help out?

BRIAN: Writing a video game definitely helped, because I learned the very curious mind of the game developer. It's not too different than our minds as comic creators, but it has a unique feel to it. I could understand the subliminal language that was being spoken. I also knew going in that these guys were very, very serious about *Halo* the way we are very, very serious about the Marvel Universe. So I understood and respected it. I think they felt that from us. When the first script came in they saw that I wasn't jerking around. They saw that I respected them and they respected that. There's always a fear that some outside guy would come in and not treat it well.

The other thing is that, because I worked on a video game and am working on one now, there are obvious differences between games and comics, but there are also more subtle differences and I when I sat down to write *Halo: Uprising* I knew about the subtleties and thought about what we could accomplish in comics that couldn't be covered in the game, because it's a point of view shooter. I wanted to give people something they couldn't get in the game instead of trying to compete with the game. We can use different narrative techniques and different voicings.

SPOTLIGHT: What seems like even more of a departure for you is that this is full-on "space alien" science fiction.

BRIAN: It's definitely hardcore sci-fi. But there is a genuinely large amount of science fiction in the books we do at Marvel. *Fantastic Four* is a super hero book because we call it a super hero book. If we called it a sci-fi book, that would be a fine label for it, too. It started off as a sci-fi/monster comic. Peter Parker getting bitten by a radioactive (or genetically modified) spider is science fiction.

But there is a different mindset to get into for this alien invasion stuff. Reading Eric Nylund's *Halo* novels helps. It's not a genre I'm unfamiliar with. I was pretty knee deep in it but coming from a different angle and to take this sci-fi genre and try to do new things with it the way we've tried with super heroes is our goal.

SPOTLIGHT: It's funny that this book is coming out now,

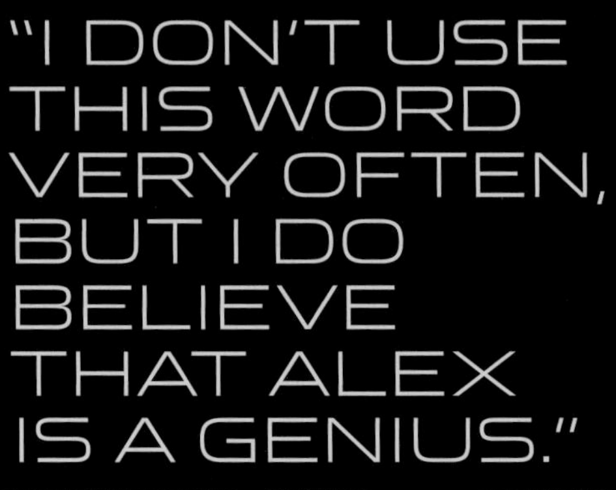
"I DON'T USE THIS WORD VERY OFTEN, BUT I DO BELIEVE THAT ALEX IS A GENIUS."

because of what just happened in *New Avengers*, which you write. Everyone knew you had something brewing and in that book and there was plenty of speculation about what would be revealed concerning the ongoing SHIELD/Hydra/Hand/Avengers conspiracy - but we all certainly thought it would be coming from an espionage angle. To reveal that Marvel's oldest aliens, the Skrulls, were behind it was very unexpected and really cool. Out of seemingly nowhere, Bendis is taking the Avengers in a sci-fi direction!

BRIAN: So yeah, I've been secretly working in hardcore sci-fi for a while! Although we are trying to turn it on its ear a little in *Avengers*. So between that and the *Illuminati* series, which has been full of large cosmic Marvel ideas, as well as a sci-fi project I was doing for a studio (that's not going to see the light of day) my head was pretty entrenched in sci-fi right around the time this came up. That was probably why I immediately thought, "Oh, hey, I could do this!" I was already kind of training myself for it.

SPOTLIGHT: So you've been in your sci-fi phase. Maybe in a few years...romance?

BRIAN: Westerns! Jewish Westerns! (*Laughter.*)

SPOTLIGHT: After *Halo: Uprising* concludes, are you planning on doing any more *Halo* stories?

BRIAN: Not right now. For Alex and I, this was like a lovely detour before we start *Spider-Woman*, which is what we were supposed to be doing before *Halo* came along. That got delayed because of some Skrull "issues." We wanted to wait to tell her story and we had a few months to kill and this came up at the same time. We're also planning a creator-owned book for the Icon line.

SPOTLIGHT: What was your experience writing the *Ultimate Spider-Man* game with Brian Reed?

MAN WITHOUT FEAR: Daredevil takes on Bullseye in Bendis/Maleev's *Daredevil #79*.

BRIAN: That was excellent. It was kind of like being paid to go to college because these guys – Brian and Chris Duffy and the people at Activision – taught me so much. Activision had gotten the rights to the *USM* game. We were at one of the smaller creator retreats and the Activision guys were there. It was a secret surprise that they were going to do Ultimate games. They were deciding on which to do and they finally settled on *Ultimate Spider-Man* and they hired me and Mark Bagley to work on it.

It was like being trained while being paid. I was being trained by these guys who really understood and who were into teaching me and helping me. It was a great experience. It actually has accentuated my experience writing the *Ultimate Spider-Man* comic to this day.

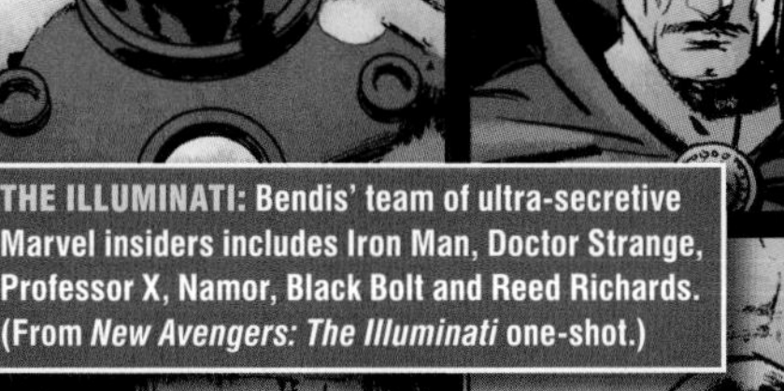

THE ILLUMINATI: Bendis' team of ultra-secretive Marvel insiders includes Iron Man, Doctor Strange, Professor X, Namor, Black Bolt and Reed Richards. (From *New Avengers: The Illuminati* one-shot.)

SPOTLIGHT: Let's talk about some other recent work you've done with Alex. But first, how did you two hook up?

BRIAN: It's funny, because Todd McFarlane (Top Cow) just released a collection of our work on *Sam and Twitch*, which is where we first met. I was a huge fan of his stuff. Alex was working on *The Crow* and I loved his stuff. *Loved* it. I whined and cried and carried on until Todd hired him on *Sam and Twitch* with me. We did five issues and I got canned. I then moved to *Daredevil* and Joe Quesada hired Alex to do it with me. It was on *Daredevil* that I learned that Alex could do anything. I don't use this word very often, but I do believe that Alex is a genius, and on many levels. When people learn that most of his art is composed digitally and that there is no actual line work, it's startling to some people.

But *Daredevil* had a style we had to stick to through most of the series because it has a consistent, pulp style. Once our run was over I definitely thought that on the next project we do, we should open Alex up and let him do other stuff.

SPOTLIGHT: The first thing you did after *Daredevil* was the *New Avengers: The Illuminati* one-shot. That was a lot less gritty than *Daredevil*.

BRIAN: That book was hand drawn, so it looked totally different. He hadn't done that at all. I told him about this idea I had about this secret grouping of heroes and there was going to be this one-shot special about them. Sometimes he gets averse to super hero stuff; he doesn't want to do something cheesy. But I told him what this was about, how it was like the Marvel Universe version of the Skull and Bones Society, or some secret group who meet in a room and control the direction of the world. It would be the perfect "shake off *Daredevil*" book. It's everything DD is not. I told him it would be great for showing people how diverse he was. He did it beautifully. Alex's artwork has a nobility to it that the book called for. And his work really has an air of conspiracy.

SPOTLIGHT: Yes. It always seems like someone off-panel besides you is watching what's going on.

BRIAN: And another thing he does around that - and he and Mark Bagley both do this so well – is he can portray an emotion on the face that is contradictory to the emotion that's expressed verbally. They give it subtext with their expressions. That is very difficult to do but they both pull it off and that is exactly what was needed for the *Illuminati* special.

SPOTLIGHT: Was the elite secret society of the Illuminati, something you've continued in the ***New Avengers: The Illuminati*** series with Jim Cheung, something you had thought up a while back?

BRIAN: Not especially. When I came up with the idea I was pumped. But of course you have this thought of "Has this been done before?" When you learn it hadn't you get so excited! Here's this new way to pull the toys out of the toy box. I was excited and everyone on editorial was excited. We debuted it in *New Avengers* because we thought the Sentry would be the perfect reason for them to get together. Then we put down the flag that they've been getting together for years. Readers got excited and then the Illuminati became the lynchpin for *Civil War* and *Planet Hulk/World War Hulk*, which I'm so proud of. Then the special came out and the reaction was huge. That revealed how they came together, and through stuff that's going on now we see how they end, and the current limited series shows stuff they did while they were together.

SPOTLIGHT: The best thing in that special was your voicing of Namor. It must have been so fun to write that.

BRIAN: There are a few characters like that at Marvel but he is the original. He'll say anything he's thinking. It's the most obnoxious thing you've heard all day, but he's not wrong! And you're gonna listen because he is a king.

HALO: UPRISING WHY STOP THERE?

Halo has been such a success as a comic, and Brian obviously had so much fun writing *Halo: Uprising*, we at *Marvel Spotlight* think he should take a break from the super hero genre and just write video game comics! We asked Brian to pitch us a few comics based on some classic '80s video games. It was tricky, but we came up with a couple of winners!

SPOTLIGHT: Howzabout writing a comic about *Frogger*?

BRIAN: *Frogger*?!? Heh heh. I was just playing that with my kid, actually. Well, we never really got any back-story on the Frogger. We don't know where he came from, where he's going. I would rewind the book and show us *why* he has to get across the street - why *that* street, you know? There's so much going on on that street, there's got to be another way to get there!

SPOTLIGHT: *Burger Time?* (Could be a good fast-food toy tie-in with that one!)

BRIAN: Was that a *Burger King* game? I'm a McDonald's fan.

SPOTLIGHT: OK, "Supersize Me"...sounds like you're ready for *Crazy Climber*?

BRIAN: Huh?

SPOTLIGHT: You're not familiar with *Crazy Climber*?

BRIAN: No!

SPOTLIGHT: I'm telling you, it would make a great comic!

BRIAN: I've never even heard of it. I liked *Gorf* or *Defender*! What needs a comic is *Geometry Wars*. We really need to find out how we got here, how all that happened. You ever play *Geometry Wars*?

SPOTLIGHT: No. I think you're making that up.

BRIAN: Oh, you gotta play it, man! It's a big Xbox thing. It's hilarious.

SPOTLIGHT: How about a comic for *Dig Dug*?

BRIAN: You are silly. I've never played that, but you are speaking a language I understand now. I've heard of that. *Crazy Climber* I think *you* just made up! How about *Smash TV*?

SPOTLIGHT: Never heard of it.

BRIAN: We obviously grew up in different parts of the country! I know – *Q*Bert* needs a comic!

SPOTLIGHT: Oh, that's good! Let's hear it!

BRIAN: I'm convinced that *Q*Bert* was some kind of mass hypnosis thing the government put out there to test us. So I'd tell that story – the story of the man who invented *Q*Bert* and what exactly his problem was, that he would see the world like this - and what it's like to inflict something that horrible on society. So it wouldn't be so much an adaptation of *Q*Bert* but more like the *Good Shepherd* version of how the *Q*Bert* came to be.

SPOTLIGHT: With the conspiracy aspects, you'd have to get Alex to draw that, too!

BRIAN: Mm hmm. Absolutely.

*Okay! Sounds pretty decisive to me. Look for a Q*BERT comic from the all-star team of Bendis and Maleev sometime in...well...never, actually!*

CASUALTIES OF A CIVIL WAR: Iron Man and Cap meet for the last time in Bendis/Maleev's *Civil War: The Confession.*

SPOTLIGHT: Namor saying, "You're a fool and here's why" to Iron Man is the best example of that.

BRIAN: Exactly. We have an issue of the limited series coming up where Dr. Strange has been dumped by Clea and they get together and start complaining about women, just like any group of men does from time to time, and Namor starts lecturing Reed about Sue! Maybe the most annoying thing ever! This guy who's tried to steal my wife lecturing me about how to keep her!

SPOTLIGHT: Sounds terrific. The next thing you did with Alex was the beautiful *New Avengers #26*: "The Ballad of Clint Barton and Wanda Maximoff."

BRIAN: *New Avengers #26* returned Hawkeye to the Marvel Universe and stopped the death threats I'd been getting, and also showed what happened to the Scarlet Witch post-*House of M*. I showed the story to Alex and his decision to illustrate it like a modern fairy tale was such a good idea. The glow that book has is so different from *Daredevil*. It really did show people that Alex really has more than one style.

SPOTLIGHT: One of the interesting things about the Hawkeye situation is that just before you "killed" him, he had starred in his own monthly book that didn't sell at all. People didn't love him until he was taken away from them, and that's a pretty good accomplishment.

BRIAN: The outcry didn't surprise me because every character is someone's favorite. I learned that lesson in *Daredevil* with the White Tiger. We killed the White Tiger in our DD run. I used the White Tiger to show Matt his "worst case scenario" if his secret

identity case ever went to trial. I was trying to catch up on White Tiger info and there was so little out there. There wasn't even a Wikipedia entry at the time. Then I learned he hadn't appeared in a comic since *1981*! So I figured, "I'm good on this. I can whack this guy and nobody'll care." He dies in the third issue of the story. So the first issue comes out and he makes this heroic return. We got literally dozens of letters: "Thank you so much for bringing back the White Tiger! He's the only Hispanic Marvel super hero and we're so glad he's back!" Meanwhile I've already killed him! It just hasn't shipped yet. So of course I got more letters...

So it's not like I'm going out of my way to tick people off, but if you manhandle these characters, you're gonna hear from people. I knew with Hawkeye, there was gonna be trouble. When we were discussing *Avengers Disassembled,* I said, "Boy, if we're gonna do this right we have to whack somebody." I'd been through this before and instead of trying to convince Marvel to let me kill this or that character, I asked for a list of who I could kill. Spare me some whining. They gave me the list and Hawkeye was on the list and I was startled. The rest of the list didn't startle me but he did. I hemmed and hawed about it for months. All of my friends kept saying, "You gotta do it!" I knew it would be shocking because *I* was shocked. But the outcry was bigger than I expected.

I mean, the reason they said I could kill him was, yeah, he had just had a solo series out that was disastrously low-selling. Not to dis the people who worked on the book; it's just that no one cared. I would hear from people who said they loved Hawkeye but hadn't bought his book. I said, "You killed him! I just put him out of his misery!"

SPOTLIGHT: The third of your trio of stories with Alex was *Civil War: The Confession*, sort of an epilogue to *Civil War* that is essentially two powerful scenes post-*CW* between Iron Man and Captain America, although in one of them, Cap is dead.

BRIAN: Yeah. It was a cool bit of synergy in that the *Illuminati* special sort of launched *Civil War* and *The Confession* is like an epilogue to it. *The Confession* got to be the emotional finale. Visually and thematically it was the perfect endcap.

The Confession came about because there were some story beats about Iron Man that we all knew about but, in a weird way, these beats - these motivations and emotions - were never spoken in the *Civil War* books. People were really hating Iron Man and seeing him as a villain. I felt it was because there were things that were not spoken out loud. [*Civil War* writer] Mark Millar and the other writers, myself included, were right not to voice it during the war because there was nowhere character-wise for him to do that. It was the middle of a war; there wasn't time for him to be emotional.

"IT'S NOT LIKE I'M GOING OUT OF MY WAY TO TICK PEOPLE OFF, BUT IF YOU MANHANDLE THESE CHARACTERS, YOU'RE GONNA HEAR FROM PEOPLE. I KNEW WITH HAWKEYE, THERE WAS GONNA BE TROUBLE."

Once Cap had died we had a meeting and I said, "That'd be a great scene if we had Tony saying all of this stuff he hadn't said and we don't know who he's talking to and we pull back and it's Cap's dead body" - and all of a sudden I had just pitched a book I was writing, whether I liked it or not! I asked Alex to do it because it was very emotional, very serious, and that's Alex. And that first half, which he colored himself, was just staggering. At that meeting I sketched out the reveal of Cap's body. I didn't show it to Alex, but he drew it almost the exact same way. That's why I love Alex. I could envision what he would do and he did it.

As always, Brian Michael Bendis' enthusiasm for writing comic books proves infectious. Thanks so much to the busy writer, husband, father and by all accounts dismal Halo *gamer for making time to talk to* Spotlight!

INSIDE THE HALO GRAPHIC NOVEL

The *Halo Graphic Novel*, Bungie's first foray into graphic storytelling with Marvel, came out in the summer of 2006. It debuted at that year's San Diego Comic-Con and sold out almost immediately upon its unveiling, becoming the talk of the convention. After its direct release to the overall marketplace, the *Halo Graphic Novel* proved to be a smash success for Marvel and Bungie as *Halo* fans lined up to check out the first work of graphic fiction set in the world of their favorite game. Here's what they found inside.

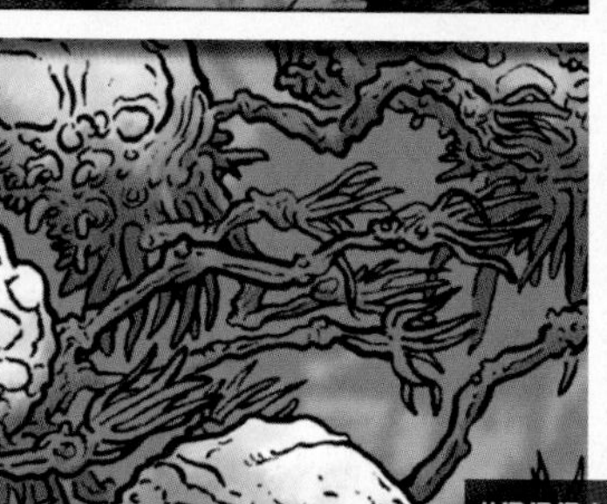

"THE LAST VOYAGE OF THE INFINITE SUCCOR"

By Lee Hammock and Simon Bisley

The Covenant face off against the threat of the Flood. A Special Ops Commander leads a crew aboard a compromised supply ship, and thanks to Bisley's splatter-iffic art, the grotesque nature of the Flood is brought to terrifying life.

"BREAKING QUARANTINE"

By Tsutomu Nihei

This suspenseful "silent" story (no dialogue or narration) pits Sgt. Johnson against the unholy menace of the Flood. It gives us the back-story of the character's heroic escape - just the sort of thing the graphic novel was designed to do: tell stories within the story!

"SECOND SUNRISE OVER NEW MOMBASA"

By Brett Lewis and Jean "Moebius" Giraud

The legendary Moebius illustrates this action packed tale featuring the citizens of New Mombasa defending their proud city in the days before it was the ghost town *Halo* players now recognize. It's another example of showing the humanity behind the game's story.

IT'S JUST CLEARING A PATH FOR THE REAL ATTACK...

"ARMOR TESTING"

By Jay Faerber, Ed Lee and Andrew Robinson

This piece opens up the story behind the Spartan armor a little bit: what went into testing it and what kind of person volunteers for this most deadly of jobs?

HRK!

the HALO effect

An interview with artist ALEX MALEEV

AFTER ONE OF THE ALL-TIME GREAT *DAREDEVIL* RUNS AND TWO PIVOTAL *CIVIL WAR* ONE-SHOTS, ARTIST ALEX MALEEV REUNITES WITH BRIAN MICHAEL BENDIS ON *HALO: UPRISING!* BY DUGAN TRODGLEN

Alex Maleev is one of the most distinctive and expressive artists in comics. His unconventional style – largely the result of a mysterious digital process – balances photo-realism with true comic book dynamics. Add to this a sharp sense of design (he received a degree in printmaking in his native Bulgaria), and you have an artist who is creating some of the most exciting pages in the industry. • His first Marvel work was his acclaimed run on *Daredevil* with his *Halo: Uprising* partner Brian Michael Bendis, with whom he had first collaborated on the Image title *Sam and Twitch*. In fact, all of Alex's Marvel work has seen him team up with his good friend Bendis. This has included a trio of modern classics: *New Avengers: The Illuminati*, *New Avengers #26*, and *Civil War: The Confession*. These comics moved Alex out of the gritty crime world of *Daredevil* and square into the middle of bigger than life super-heroics, and he showed he could excel equally in this milieu. • Next up is a sharp turn in yet another direction: a limited series based on the sci-fi video game phenomenon *Halo*. Alex has also done storyboards for films like *The Bone Collector* and has provided some of Sylar's paintings on the NBC hit *Heroes*. *Spotlight* asked Alex about his previous work and what it's like to draw a comic based on a game.

SPOTLIGHT: Growing up in Bulgaria, did you have access to US comics? What do you recall about them?

ALEX: There wasn't much access. Behind the Iron Curtain, any Western literature was subjected to tight filtering under the "everythingthatcomesfromtheWest-iscorrupt" guidelines. Somehow a French magazine called *PIF* made it through and I bought as many as I could. Marvel and DC were virtually unknown.

SPOTLIGHT: You attended art school and seem to have influences well beyond comic book art. Did you see yourself getting into the comics industry?

ALEX: Not at the time. My art aspirations were strictly in the etching/lithography field. Comics invaded my life much later.

SPOTLIGHT: What does your formal art/printmaking training bring to your comic work?

ALEX: As much as possible. It surely plays a big role in the way I draw and its influences could still be found in current work. It surely was a determining factor in my *Daredevil* run.

SPOTLIGHT: After getting your degree, you still attended the Joe Kubert School. What made you decide you wanted to do this and how did it affect your work?

ALEX: (The Kubert School) was my ticket to the US as it provided me with a student visa. I quit four months later to try my luck in New York City.

SPOTLIGHT: Was going from lithography to the storytelling aspects of comic book art difficult? Fun?

ALEX: Storytelling is in the roots of many pieces of artwork and since my etchings were very illustrative, the transition was silky smooth. I just had to break it down in panels after learning some basic rules about comic book layouts. Working as a storyboard artist for some major pictures and having the chance to be "schooled" by some great directors certainly helped, too.

SPOTLIGHT: How did you end hooking

ALEX: Todd McFarlane put us together. (Thanks Todd, you know I am eternally grateful for it.)

SPOTLIGHT: How did you hook up with McFarlane in the first place?

ALEX: He called me.

SPOTLIGHT: Did you consider the *Daredevil* gig a big turning point? A moment when you knew you had "arrived" in the industry?

ALEX: I didn't know what to expect, but after *Sam and Twitch* I felt I could do anything with Brian, that's how comfortable I felt. *Halo: Uprising* is a solid proof of our mutual trust.

SPOTLIGHT: Did the legacy of *Daredevil*, particularly that of Frank Miller, weigh on you at all?

ALEX: With all due respect to Frank Miller, absolutely not. I felt no pressure at all, my job was to draw at the best at my abilities and hand in the pages on time. How our book is going to be perceived in the future compared to Frank's, Joe's, or any other DD run is not up to me to determine.

SPOTLIGHT: You have a unique tech-

"IT'S VERY TRICKY AS I HAVE A CHARACTER IN ARMOR THE WHOLE TIME. CONVEYING THE EMOTIONS IS HEAVILY DEPENDENT ON BODY LANGUAGE, SURROUNDING SUPPORTING CAST AND ENVIRONMENT."

– ALEX MALEEV, ON DRAWING *HALO*'S MASTER CHIEF

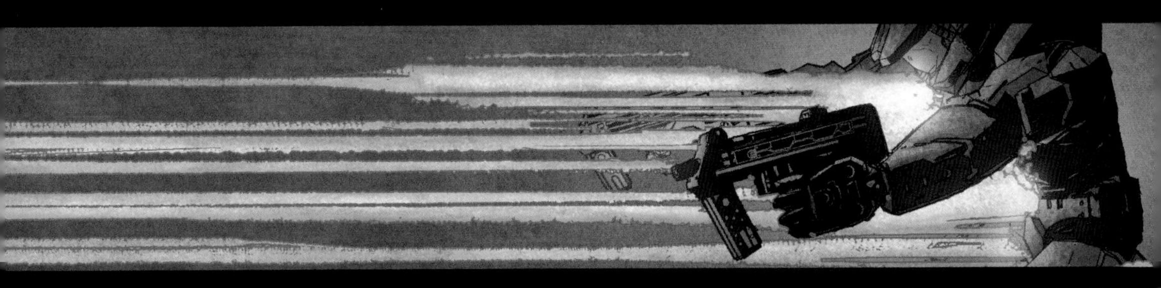

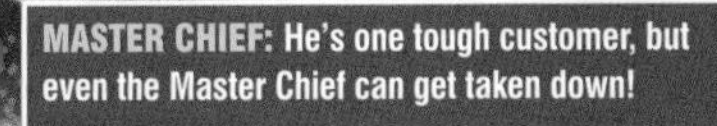

MASTER CHIEF: He's one tough customer, but even the Master Chief can get taken down!

HOUSE OF MALEEV: Alex Maleev's stunning design in *New Avengers #26* added a dreamlike quality to the return of Hawkeye and Scarlet Witch.

nique, with photo-realism and a keen design sense. Describe your process and how it developed.

ALEX: Ha-ha.

SPOTLIGHT: What have your colorists Matt Hollingsworth and Dave Stewart brought to your work? How closely do you collaborate?

ALEX: I have close relationships with both and have been very fortunate to be teamed up with them. Hollingsworth is a close friend of mine as well and having him on *Halo* is a reunion in heaven!

SPOTLIGHT: Your *New Avengers: The Illuminati* special with Brian had a new look to it. How did you approach this one differently?

ALEX: It needed to be done in '60s-70's style and I tried to stay as close and as true as I could to the comic artwork from that era. (Tip of the hat to Neil Adams, whose Avengers are amazing and were at my desk the whole time I was drawing *Illuminati*.)

SPOTLIGHT: You actually penciled *Illuminati* by hand. Was this the first time you had produced a comic this way?

ALEX: Most of it, maybe 2-3 pages were done digitally. I started working on a computer halfway through *Sam and Twitch*, but everything before that was old school.

SPOTLIGHT: You then collaborated with Brian on the beautiful *New Avengers #26*. Especially your painted cover, which is one for the ages. Was your Scarlet Witch inspired by anything in particular? Klimt, I assume?

ALEX: Klimt and the late Dino Battaglia, an Italian illustrator not very well known in the States. It's a shame, as I believe

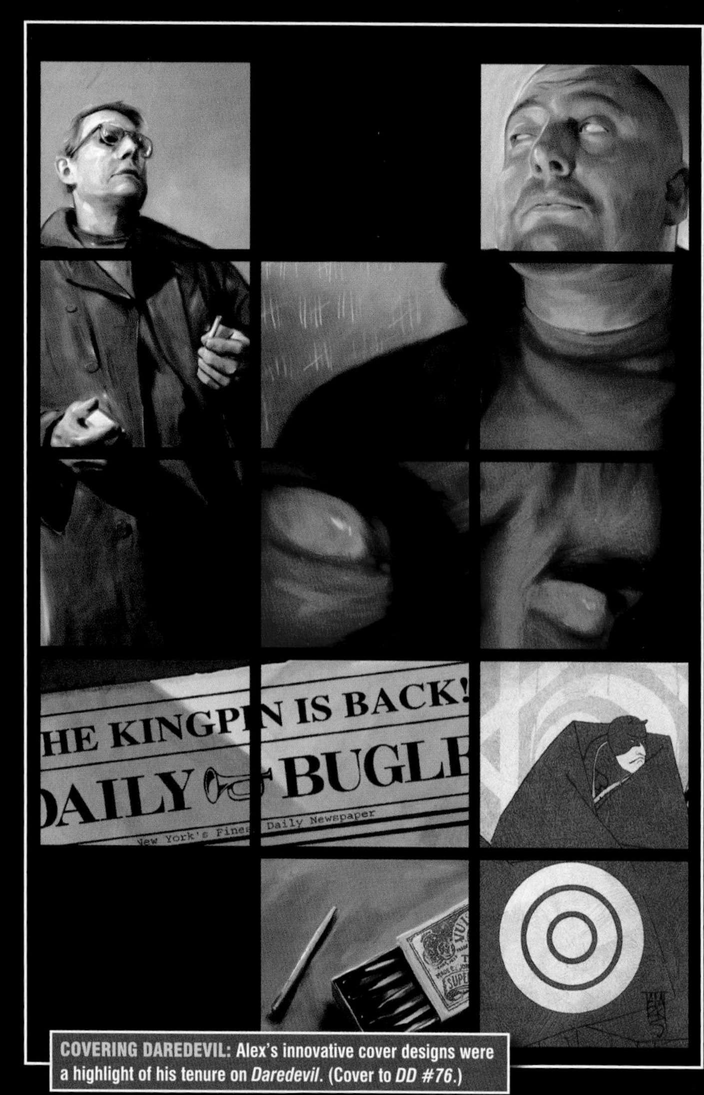

COVERING DAREDEVIL: Alex's innovative cover designs were a highlight of his tenure on *Daredevil*. (Cover to *DD #76*.)

ne was one of the finest artists in our industry. Please look him up, and you will notice the resemblance in the first half *of New Avengers #26*. This book was a tribute to both of these masters.

SPOTLIGHT: You colored this issue yourself and the results were fantastic. It looks like your pencils are looser knowing you'd be finishing it yourself with colors.

ALEX: The results were not near what I wanted, but I hope the trade will serve justice to the colors.

SPOTLIGHT: Despite your strong work in the world of the Avengers, Brian says you are reluctant to enter the work with traditional super heroes too much. Why is that?

ALEX: I don't wanna take the bread from the table of my famous colleagues. (*Laughter.*) I feel comfortable in the dark and greedy corner looking at the bright picture, but every once in a blue moon I have to put my name on something larger and *Halo* is such a stage for artistic and professional growth.

THE SEEDS OF A *CIVIL WAR*: This evocative image from the *Illuminati* one-shot heralded things to come in comics' biggest event, *Civil War*.

SPOTLIGHT: Now you're working on *Halo: Uprising*. Are you a *Halo* fan or a video game fan at all? Brian says you are actually something of a master on *Halo 2*. Accurate?

ALEX: I wish. Kids half my age kick my butt regularly. I have my moments of brilliance, but they are random. I can't play as much (as I would like); I do have a job, you know?

SPOTLIGHT: As a *Halo* fan, was it exciting to be approached to so the book? Unexpected?

ALEX: I knew it was coming. It was an idea brewed long ago and it even took longer to happen than we expected.

SPOTLIGHT: Does this sort of adaptation provide some unique challenges?

ALEX: It's very tricky as I have a character in armor the whole time. Conveying the emotions is heavily dependent on body language, surrounding support-

tricks from the bag on that one.

SPOTLIGHT: Does the look of the game go into your design sense for the story?

ALEX: Very much so. I wanna stay faithful to all gamers out there who love slaying.

SPOTLIGHT: How close to Brian's scripts do you stay? Do you consult him on changes you want to make?

ALEX: Very close. It's been that way since the beginning. I rarely alter stuff and when I do I run it by him. I have great respect for his writing and my job is to bring it to life.

SPOTLIGHT: The *Halo* graphic novel sold to a great number of people who otherwise were not comic book buyers, and thus served as an ambassador of sorts to the world of com-

this. Does that come with a sense of responsibility?

ALEX: Same as the Frank Miller question. My sole responsibility is stay on top of my game and constantly try to improve.

SPOTLIGHT: *Halo* doesn't have the history of moody, cathartic art like *Daredevil*; it might have less super hero conventions than other Marvel books. Does the nature of this book affect your approach at all?

ALEX: Definitely. I look at this project with different eyes. These two books are not compatible at all and my approach is in accordance to the new challenges.

Alex is obviously one of the most dedicated comic book artists around. Thanks to Alex for letting us inside his head a little bit. Look for Alex's dynamite

WAITING FOR THE FLOOD

HALO NATION COMES TO MARVEL

AS *HALO: UPRISING* UNVEILS THE TRANSITION FROM *HALO 2* TO *HALO 3*, BUNGIE STUDIO'S BRIAN JARRARD AND MICROSOFT'S FRANK O'CONNOR GET US ALL CAUGHT UP WITH THIS INTERVIEW FROM 2007 ABOUT WHAT IT'S LIKE TO SHARE AN OFFICE WITH THE MASTER CHIEF.

BY JOHN RHETT THOMAS

In the first half of *Marvel Spotlight*, we checked in with Bendis and Maleev, the creative duo bringing Marvel-style comic storytelling to *Halo*. Now, we open the floor to Brian Jarrard and Frank O'Connor, two gentlemen who have helped bring the high-octane actions and suspense of *Halo* to Marvel! Both veterans of *Halo*, Brian and Frank are insiders of the best kind: capable, creative, and totally in love with the product they're producing. • Brian's current job title is Community Director for Bungie - a liaison for the *Halo* fan community, which is perhaps the easiest part of his job (it takes a fan to know a fan, after all!) He also seeks to expand the *Halo* franchise into new and exciting ventures – like Marvel Comics! • Frank worked his way from writing for video game magazines all the way to recently becoming Halo Franchise Development Director for Microsoft Game Studios. His job: craft the story narratives that underpin new action in the *Halo* universe, and also work a little wordsmith-ing magic in licensed *Halo* fiction! • Both these men find their work to be both exciting and fulfilling in ways that neither could have possibly known would lie in store for them. We checked in with them in 2007, before the launch of *Halo 3*, to find out what living 24/7 in the world of *Halo* was like!

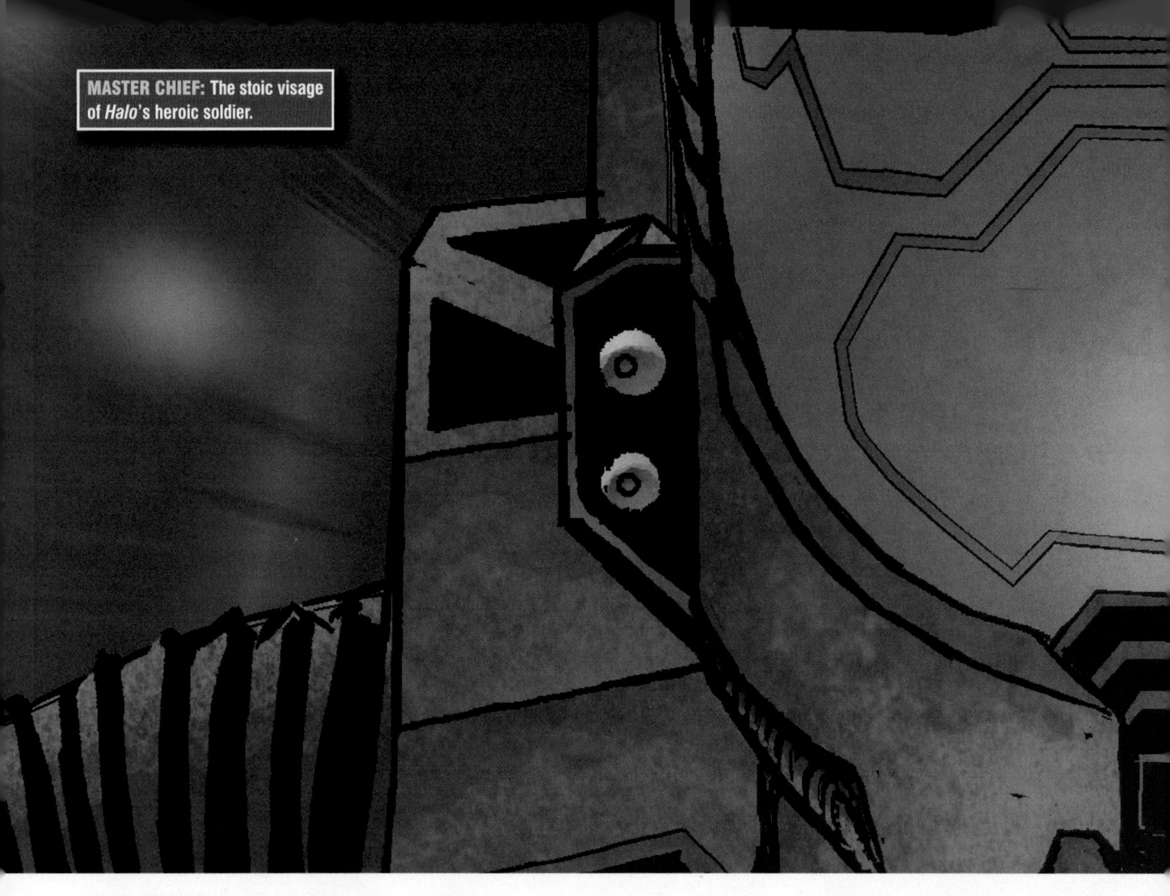

MASTER CHIEF: The stoic visage of *Halo*'s heroic soldier.

SPOTLIGHT: Were either of you much interested in comic books or graphic storytelling before you got involved with Marvel on the *Halo* project?

BRIAN: Back in the day I was a huge fan of comics, but over the years I had less and less time to actively read and collect them. I used to read everything out there – nowadays it's the occasional graphic novel here or there and since we've been working with Marvel, I had a chance to get back into their universe with *Civil War* and some of Alex and Brian's previous work. Almost everyone on our team enjoys some form of comics to this day and we were always interested in finding ways to take *Halo* into this medium in a way that wasn't just a licensed spinoff trying to cash-in on *Halo*. *Halo* is known for its great fiction and awesome visuals – two things that are a natural fit for comics.

FRANK: I have always been a huge comics fan. From childhood, I'd read imported Marvel comics – they printed them in the UK on a weird landscape format that's probably pretty collectible now, but also likely wrecked the artist's original layout scheme. I never noticed – I simply immersed myself in *Spider-Man*, *Hulk*, *Nova*...you name it. Growing up in Scotland, I was jealous that I was unable to mail order those amazing Sea Monkeys you guys played with for hours. How I envied you, with your undersea kingdom of fantasy and delight. My favorite comic book hero, perhaps coincidentally, was Namor. His disdain for puny mortals was my favorite element.

SPOTLIGHT: Following the success of last year's original graphic novel, *Halo* is once again being adapted into comic book form. Many comic book fans may not be familiar with *Halo*, so can you give a quick synopsis of the story elements behind the video game that you think are important for new readers to understand?

BRIAN: Halo has a really deep universe behind it that goes far beyond just the games. However, the most important thing to understand is that in the distant future, a technologically superior evil alien collective known as the Covenant is hell bent on wiping out humanity on their way to achieving what they hope is "the Great Journey." Their religious beliefs, based on an ancient and mysterious race known as the "The Forerunners" has led them all over the galaxy in search of clues and artifacts and along the way they are exterminating mankind. Mankind's only hope was to develop the ultimate weapon – the Spartans.

These cybernetically enhanced super soldiers were initiated into a life of military training and service from childhood and equipped with MJOLNIR armor giving them superhuman abilities. They were effective but ultimately the Covenant wiped out the Spartan program and nearly all were killed. One surviving Spartan, John-117, aka The Master Chief, is now humanity's last hope to stop the Covenant from destroying everything. And on top of it all – a new, more deadly foe was uncovered during the events of the first Halo game. A sentient parasitic species known as "The Flood" that is more terrifying and potentially more devastating than anything the Covenant could throw at us. Master Chief and his allies now face a battle on two fronts and the fate of the galaxy and all mankind hangs in the balance.

FRANK: Cue explosions, heroism and sweet jumps.

SPOTLIGHT: Can you delve into the community built up behind the video

"[MEMBERS OF HALO NATION] FILL EVERY NICHE OF THE DEMOGRAPHIC SPECTRUM: DOCTORS, SOLDIERS, ATHLETES, KIDS, MOMS, YOU NAME IT."

— GAME WRITER FRANK O'CONNOR

game and its players, how that came to be, and how games like *Halo* help fulfill the promise of terms like "virtual reality," (and, boy, doesn't that seem like such a 20th Century term by now, what with all the technological advancements of each new year?)

FRANK: The Halo community, or "Halo Nation" as the marketing guys call it, is a collection of folks with a common interest in playing, reading about and collecting *Halo* stuff. Beyond that they fill every niche of the demographic spectrum. Doctors, soldiers, athletes, kids, moms, you name it. As for virtual reality, *Halo* does allow the player some real escapism – the chance to go to a new and amazing place, and more importantly, to go there and be a superhero.

BRIAN: For some, who have logged thousands of hours online, this is a big part of their reality. Legions of fans are drawn together by the story, the characters, the conflict but there are others who only love *Halo* for the online experience and competition of playing against others for top honors.

SPOTLIGHT: *Halo* is arguably as influential today as *Star Wars* was back in the '70s and '80s. Video games are still a bit off the radar from the culture at large, but with broadband internet becoming more ubiquitous in homes and internet cafes across the world, gaming consoles like the Xbox are slowly occupying the place that movie theaters hold as the arbiters of cultural momentum. What do you think of that assessment of *Halo*'s place in popular culture? And if you think it's valid, what are your reflections as part of its spearhead?

BRIAN: The *Star Wars* analogy is used a lot but rightly so – it's the closest thing we have, in broad terms, to help mainstream society understand why this "game" is such a big deal. That's a lofty goal and clearly *Halo* is not as big as *Star Wars* or some of the behemoth movie-based entertainment properties but clearly it's more than "just a game" at this point. With over 15 million games sold, nearly 1 billion hours logged on Xbox for *Halo 2* and critically acclaimed best-selling novels, and a great graphic novel, *Halo* is cultural phenomenon that is only just getting started.

FRANK: Comparing *Halo* to *Star Wars* is cool, and an honor – but the two phenomena exist at very different scales. We dream of being as popular as *Star Wars*, but that's about it. They do have one or two things in common though – like memorable vehicles and weapons, and archetypal characters with whom you can easily relate. *Halo's* different however, in that you kind of make your own stories during gameplay and enjoy and remember your own moments. We're adding a saved films functionality so that folks can make that experience a little more literal this time around. Maybe we'll create some budding George Lucases.

SPOTLIGHT: Do you think that *Halo*has had more of a "stealth effect" than *Star Wars* in achieving its level of influence on pop culture?

BRIAN: For the Bungie team, it's all a bit surreal – nobody expected *Halo* to become the juggernaut that it is today. The team knew the game was fun to play, the story was compelling, the characters were interesting... but nobody would've thought *Halo* could become as big as it has in recent years. If by "stealth effect" you are referring to its gradual rise in awareness and fame – absolutely. *Star Wars* exploded onto the big screen and the world was never the same. *Halo* exploded onto Xbox over five years ago and has been slowly growing and expanding ever since until it finally broke out of the videogame mold and garnered real mainstream recognition.

HOSTAGE TO THE JACKALS: Ruwan and Myras are forced to stand down as the Covenant take over.

SPOTLIGHT: Did anybody involved in the early development of *Halo* foresee its evolution into the sophisticated cultural community it has become? Or has this evolution been somewhat organic and beyond any one person's prognostication or planning?

FRANK: It's largely been a surprise until now. Bungie has had to expand and adapt to catch up with its success, but now we're set up to deal with the scale and the challenge of these products and opportunities and things like an expanded writing team, a franchise group and a larger more capable organization are all necessary elements of a mature expansion of the studio.

BRIAN: Nobody on the original Bungie team responsible for *Halo* expected the game and franchise to become what it is today. I think the real potential started to sink in as *Halo 2* was under development – when the hype and expectations were off the charts – when national news and celebrities started talking about it – that's when people started to realize what we had in front of us. Then again, Bungie Studio has always had a charter of total world domination and *Halo* is a huge step towards that end – so perhaps there was a mastermind behind it afterall.

SPOTLIGHT: From your vantage point, how was the *Halo* original graphic novel published in 2006 received by hardcore *Halo* fans? To what extent is it considered canon for the gaming experience, or was it best seen as entertainment inspired by *Halo*, but existing to some degree outside of the gaming experience?

FRANK: It's very canonical. We worked directly with all of the artists and writers to ensure that. We made some compromises for the sake of the artists' creative vision – a cape-wearing Elite and a hat with bunny ears spring to mind, but mostly we just stayed clear and let them interpret the universe with sensible guidelines in place.

BRIAN: It was a success on all levels – we were thrilled to make the book we wanted to make, with the people we wanted to make it with. Our fans were excited to get a new glimpse at different stories in the Halo Universe, told and visualized by some of the best in the industry. We try our best to make all *Halo* endeavors adhere to our story bible and consider almost all of them to be canon whether it be books or the HGN. The graphic novel stories were all shaped by our team in partnership with some really talented writers so it was most certainly intended to be canon for the games and the story we began in *Halo: Combat Evolved.*

SPOTLIGHT: Is there a desire from Bungie's side to explore more graphic novels like the *Halo OGN*? If so, what shape or form might that take?

BRIAN: The great thing about *Halo* is that there are so many potential stories to tell – so many characters to explore. We'd love to go back to another graphic novel or something of that nature but the tricky part is finding the time to make it happen. The HGN was a huge endeavor for us and it luckily came at a time when we had some time and resources available. As a Studio that is primarily focused on making games, it might be tough to find that kind of opportunity again.

SPOTLIGHT: Marvel has a long history of taking licensed properties and creating comics with the Marvel magic added to the mix. And sometimes, properties like *Conan the Barbarian, Micronauts, ROM, Transformers* and *Godzilla* have all crossed over into the Marvel Universe proper (particularly with this summer's *New Avengers/Transformers* crossover looking to be a lot of fun). Have there been any thoughts about perhaps mixing *Halo* with certain Marvel titles or

characters and looking for synergy with a similar crossover experience?

BRIAN: We have had fun discussing this from a purely hypothetical situation (a favorite being Master Chief vs. <insert any Marvel character>) but honestly I don't think it's something that would make sense for *Halo* or the Marvel Universe... but you never know, maybe someday the right circumstances would arise with the right team behind it.

FRANK: We have done precisely one crossover – a female Spartan fighter in DOA4 for Xbox 360 – and that was semi-tongue in cheek. But the trick is to never say never. Nothing on the horizon, however.

SPOTLIGHT: Discussing the playability of the game itself, how do you look back at the initial incarnation of *Halo: Combat Evolved* now nearly six years removed from its premiere? Is it kind of like looking back at Orville and Wilbur Wright's first flight while you're preparing to unveil jet aircraft flight for the first time?

FRANK: Not exactly. Orville and Wilbur Wright did something more akin to what id Software did with Wolfenstein. We've made plenty of innovations and improvements, but others did a lot of the invention long before *Halo*. If you think about what we did with controls for a console FPS then you could maybe stretch the metaphor to say we invented the Harrier jump jet. And some of the stuff we have planned for *Halo 3* might be Joint Strike Fighter-y. Now I confused myself.

SPOTLIGHT: Can you give an idea of the advancements, both from playability to narrative story elements, that will be a part of *Halo 3*?

BRIAN: There are so many new things going on in *Halo 3* it's hard to know where to begin – in every way, this is the biggest, deepest and best game Bungie Studios has ever made. From graphics to artificial intelligence to brand new features like Saved Films, we've crammed an incredible amount of new stuff into this game while still staying true to essence of *Halo*. For us, the technological advancements afforded by the Xbox 360 allow our artists to build more immersive worlds, more realistic environments that are bigger in scale and scope than ever before. We can throw more guys on screen – friend and foe – and can devote more resources to AI and an insanely deep level of sound design. All of these things add up to what we hope will be an awesome experience for *Halo* fans and gamers alike. The team is able to tell the story of *Halo 3* in a really compelling and entertaining way.

FRANK: We can't talk about the story, but we will say this: we tell a better story in a more lucid and technically impressive way, this time around. Which should be our goal for every successive iteration of anything we make.

BRIAN: On the other side we have the entire multiplayer portion of *Halo 3*. Matchmaking on Xbox Live, meeting friends, exchanging custom files, sharing in a social experience – these aspects of the game are more robust and polished than before. *Halo 2* revolutionized online gaming in a lot of ways and *Halo 3* is raising the bar even further. We've put extra emphasis this time on user-created content and tools for our community to really empower them to take *Halo* to new places and keep the game going years after its release. With Saved Films, for example, you can capture every game you play whether it be multiplayer or campaign, and play it back watching the action unfold from any angle you want and then share those films over Xbox Live. This has all sorts of awesome implications for competitive gamers who simply want to study films to get better but also for the machinima community and folks like Red vs. Blue who will no doubt use these tools to create awesome Halo content for everyone to enjoy.

SPOTLIGHT: Can you give an insider view on how the beta-testing of *Halo 3* went? Were you a part of that, and did it meet everyone's expectations?

BRIAN: Overall the Halo 3 beta test went very well for us. We had a rocky start but once the wrinkles were ironed out we

ONE AGAINST THE COVENANT: The Master Chief's last stand?

LOCKDOWN: Myras and Ruwan are among thousands taken prisoner of war in Cleveland.

had a tremendous participation and thus an incredible amount of networking and server data to help our engineers polish and fine tune the game. At last count, we had well over 800,000 unique players – far above anything we expected internally. And even though it wasn't a finished and fully polished game, the overwhelming fan response was positive – the controls felt right and it was a hell of a lot of fun to play.

FRANK: (The beta-testers) spammed us with more data than we knew what to do with. The result will be improved network code and gameplay balance for everyone when the game goes live.

SPOTLIGHT: Finally, *Halo 3* is scheduled to debut in September. Obviously, it's going to be a huge deal coming out of the gate. It promises to bring a close to the trilogy started with the first game, but in what ways will this trilogy be only the beginning? I presume there are already plans for *Halo* beyond *Halo 3*, and if so, what kind of hints can you give as to what that might entail?

BRIAN: Right now we've got our hands full finishing *Halo 3* and it really is the end of the trilogy that we started back in *Halo: Combat Evolved*. It won't be the end of the *Halo* Universe though. We can't say much more than that right now but we'll have a lot more to say when the time is right. Until then, prepare to finish the fight on September 25th!

SPOTLIGHT: Beyond *Halo*, is there anything else going on in Bungie land you'd like to pass on to readers?

BRIAN: We have all sorts of projects and plans for achieving world domination that are underway but unfortunately I'm sworn to an oath of secrecy that prevents me from divulging any details.

FRANK: Expect that *Halo 3* will be our best game yet.

Thanks to Frank and Brian for chatting with us. We'll see you in our Xbox when HALO 3 *comes out!*

- 1 Sketch Variant -

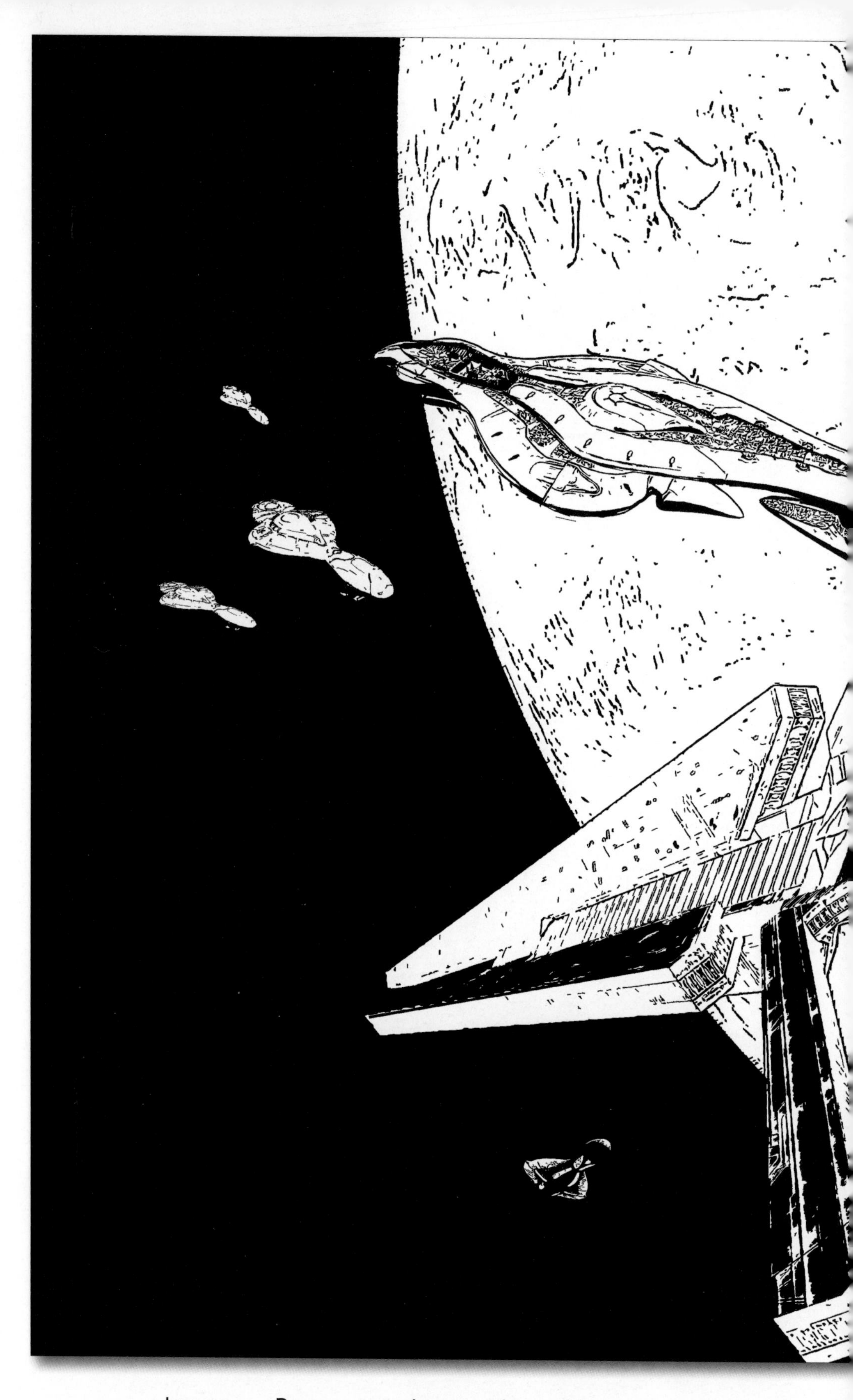

- Issue 1, Pages 2-3 Art by Alex Maleev -

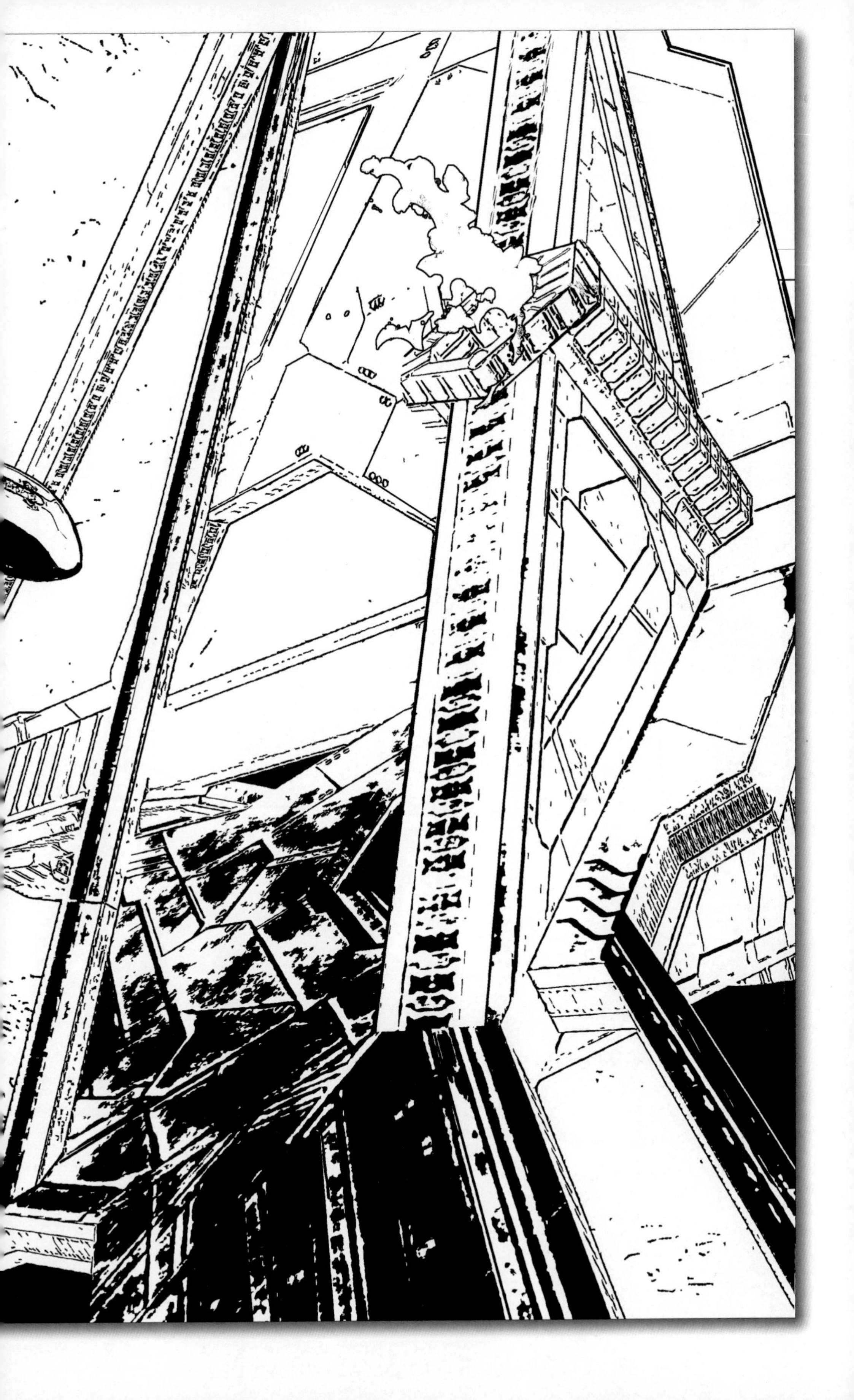

- Issue 1, Page 6 Art by Alex Maleev -

- Issue 1, Page 30 Art by Alex Maleev -

- Issue 2, Pages 9-10 Art by Alex Maleev -

- Issue 2, Page 28 Art by Alex Maleev -

- Issue 3, Page 30 Art by Alex Maleev -

- Issue 4, Page 5 Art by Alex Maleev -